BREAKING BRAIN BARRIERS

Sensory and Gender-Based Activities to Enhance Learning

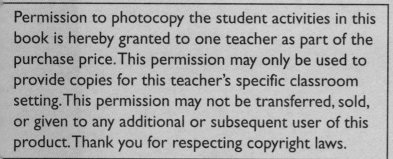

Written by Dr. Linda Karges-Bone
Illustrated by Darcy Tom and Luda Stekol
Cover design by Kati Baker and Jeff Richards
Book design by Kati Baker

Printed in the United States of America

ISBN 978-1-42911-501-8

BRIDGING
the Gaps in Education™
Lorenz Educational Press
P.O. Box 802 • Dayton, OH 45401-0802

for other LEP products visit our website
www.LorenzEducationalPress.com

Dedication

This book is for "Bone's Babies", my senior methods capstone course students at Charleston Southern University, who named themselves in this way and even brandished it proudly on a t-shirt when we formed a dodge ball team to raise money for charity. It is your spirit, passion, and commitment that motivate me to find fresh ways to "break brain barriers" and connect neural pathways for children who desperately need to feel smart, creative, and confident. Gandhi said: "Be the change you wish to see in the world" and you are living evidence of that mantra.

Message

Teachers who are called to the ministry of transforming minds will need to break down the barriers that poverty, prejudice, and power place in their way. They will need spiritual strength in order to carry out the work of "breaking brain barriers", their own and those placed in the minds of their students. That is why the job isn't for the faint of heart: "Let not many of you become teachers, my brethren, knowing that as such we will incur a stricter judgment." James 3:1. For those who persevere, I salute you.

Acknowledgements

I wish to acknowledge the work of the Single Gender Inquiry Group at Spann Elementary School in Summerville, South Carolina, who are committed to "breaking brain barriers" for children in poverty. You are pioneers and prophets! Barbara Bassett, Britt Blanton, Scott Bloom, Joanne Florencio, Shantae Gilliard, Karen Garcia, Ellen James, Rene' Jones, Brianne Peters, Nicholas Turoski, and Principal, Wanda Carroll-Williams

Table of Contents

Do Something Different in Your Classroom 4

Introduction to Sensory-Based Learning 5

Color-Based Activities 6

Scent-Based Activities 24

Taste-Based Activities 36

Touch-Based Activities 49

Sound-Based Activities 57

Introduction to Gender-Based Learning. 62

Gender-Based Activities 63

Dear Teachers and Parents,

If you are holding a copy of "Differentiated Pathways of the Brain" or "Breaking Brain Barriers", then you are already on the right neural circuit. Clearly, you believe that our brains, and I emphasize <u>brains</u> in the plural, are more unique, capable, and curious than we ever understood them to be.

Dr. Howard Gardner, of Harvard University, is acknowledged as the "mind behind the MI (multiple intelligences) theory" and it has been 26 years since the seminal text <u>Frames of Mind</u> (1983) was published. In that time, Gardner has added only one "intelligence" to the original seven, though in a recent interview, he suggests a possible 8th: "existential" intelligence. (Edutopia Interview, <u>www.edutopia.org</u> April 2009).

Over the past 26 years, evidence from neuroscience, medical imaging, and fieldwork converge and connect, affirming a model for teaching and learning that demands divergence and differentiation. Clearly, there are multiple pathways to knowledge and creativity, yet there seem to be just as many <u>barriers</u> preventing us from achieving our full potential.

I like to use this scenario to illustrate the point. Imagine that you are leaving your school this afternoon, headed home after a full, exhausting day of teaching. You enter the same freeway or interstate that you typically access and proceed at a fast clip. Suddenly, out of nowhere, with no warning, you see roadblocks and detour signs at your familiar exit. No way to get home. You think, "OK, I'll get off at the next exit and loop back." But that too, is inaccessible. In fact, 8 of 10 exits are closed and you are not allowed to know which ones are open. It is a gauntlet. Tomorrow, you hear on the radio, there will be different closings on the freeway, and again, no warnings nor maps. How frustrated would you be? How angry? How tired?

Well, that is the "Cognitive Freeway" for many students. Their prior learning experiences (or lack thereof), culture of poverty, high stress levels, lack of nurturing, few role models, or absence of fertile, literacy or artistic experiences limit their access to learning. At the same time, many teachers, who give a nod to differentiation and accommodations in theory, offer few opportunities for it in their practice. It is "their way or no highway" in the classroom. As a result, at least 50% of American high school students simply drop out of school. There is simply no way to get through the barriers to learning and creativity.

However, I believe in "Breaking Brain Barriers" by using sensory and gender-based strategies, interventions, and accommodations to open up more "exits" on the freeway. These are simple yet effective ways to connect emotions, experiences, and cognitive "events" so that students maintain focus and commit to practice long enough to put information and ideas into long-term memory.

Gardner suggests that there are many ways to be intelligent. Before him, John Dewey voiced the importance of experiences that make learning real for students. And, Dr. Maria Montessori emphasized the value of sensory-rich learning to connect the mind and the body.

"Breaking Brain Barriers" draws on all three models and adds a fourth, the component of gender-specific methods that add subtle, yet powerful changes to teaching that may accommodate boys' and girls' preferences. Whether you choose to add the scent of apple to your classroom while students practice math problems; play classical music during work time; create a competition as part of a science inquiry; or hide scented dryer sheets in the room to reduce feelings of tension is entirely up to you. The sheer willingness to make a change will probably induce some sort of positive result. Serotonin will surge as you experience pleasure in planning something new and fun for your students, and that good energy will reflect through "mirror neurons" and be caught by your students…the first step in "Breaking Brain Barriers".

Wishing You Joyful Teaching and Learning,

Linda

Dr. Linda Karges-Bone
Summerville, South Carolina
June 2009

"There is no reason algebra needs to be taught in just one way. If software exists, or can be created to teach algebra in numerous ways, what possible objection could there be to such individualization? And even when the software does not exist, there are many ways in which one can individualize-for example, by having students help one another, breaking the class into "jigsaw" groups, presenting ideas in multiple ways, and so on. I think the problem is not changing because of MI (multiple intelligences); it is changing for any reason. Most of us would prefer to do just what we've been doing before, whether or not it has worked well."

Interview with Dr. Howard Gardner conducted by Owen Edwards in <u>www.edutopia.org</u> April 2009.

Do Something Different in Your Classroom
Break Brain Barriers

Rate Your Capacity for "Breaking Brain Barriers"

Consider your lesson plans for a typical week. Using the matrix below as a guide, circle the incidences of "brain friendly" strategies or approaches that you used. Rate your capacity using the scale.

Learning styles accommodations	Stress reduction techniques	Literature connections	Application of neural architecture	Targeting emotional intelligence
Sensory-rich, tactile learning	Group sizes	Multiple intelligences	Left/right brain strategies	Infusion of color therapy
Creativity enhancement or "white space" for mind play	Tiered assessments	Challenges and competitions	Chunking and layering of standards	Pacing changes
Drama and role play	Creative movement	Thematic instruction	Use of scent to affect mood	Higher order thinking
Music and rhythms as background or tool	Gender-specific approaches	Brain foods as snacks, rewards, or manipulatives	Cooperative activities	Reading aloud
Temperature or lighting changes	Use of the color green in plants, paint, or paper	Graphic organizers for directions, study skills, practice	Use of deliberate questioning strategies: Bloom's Taxonomy	Individualized goal setting

1-3 uses - **Beginning to Break Brain Barriers**
> Add a new one next week and see how it feels. You are on the brink of real change!

4-7 uses - **Better than most at Breaking Brain Barriers**
> You are a creative, adventurous sort and have a strong sense of your ability to change brains! Continue to grow.

8 or more uses - **Beyond Brain Barriers**
> You won't let anything hold back your own creativity nor the capacity of your students. You are a role model and should use this book as a professional development tool to train others!

My Personal Goals

_____

_____

_____

Introduction to Sensory-Based Learning
Your Goal: Neural Nirvana!

There are many wonderful reasons to use sensory-rich experiences in teaching, and they are woven into the suggested strategies in this section of <u>Breaking Brain Barriers</u>. But consider one that has been neglected in our practice: sensory-rich teaching will stimulate your own rapidly aging brain, and make <u>you</u> more aware, creative, and flexible. For purely selfish reasons, begin to richly layer color, scent, taste, touch, and music into your plans and practice and revel in your newfound passion for teaching.

It makes sense to harness the senses. Teachers have always been the real reason that initiatives succeed or fail. Hundreds of well-researched, well-funded programs and projects begin with a flourish and end in a flop and three years later, nobody in the school even remembers what all the letters in the acronym stood for. Was R.E.A.L. for Realizing Every Aspect of Literacy? Or, was it Recognizing Each Avenue of Learning? Did it even matter? Unless teachers believe in a change, want to change, or commit to change.....nothing will change. I believe that teachers will embrace "Breaking Brain Barriers" because it allows for something that has been stolen from teachers by scripted curricula and rigid views of practice: the opportunity to personalize and play in their classrooms.

Whether you teach special needs children, ESL, gifted, or just garden variety, high energy kids, you can <u>break brain barriers</u>. If you are in a Head Start Program or a progressive, magnet high school, you can <u>break brain barriers</u>. Anyone who believes that there are many ways to connect neurons and nurture creativity, but who has become stymied by the high pressures of today's classrooms and learning communities, can have fun with this book and recharge his or her batteries. So, grab a can of chilled shaving cream, a box of scented markers, and a bag of peppermints and create your own "Neural Nirvana" by breaking brain barriers.

The activities in the first half of the book are arranged according to sense: color-based activities, scent-based activities, taste-based activities, touch-based activities, and sound-based activities are all included. The icons at the top of each page will help you navigate through the various sections. Even though they may be geared toward a specific sense, the activities in this book can easily be adjusted to provide a multisensory experience for the participating students.

Color and Cognition Chart

Use the chart below to help you implement color in your classroom, or in the various activities that you complete throughout the school day.

Color	\ Cognitive or Symbolic Impact				
	Excitement	Alertness	Creativity	Reflection	Relaxation
Black		X			
Blue	X Royal		X Sky	X Aqua	X Pale
Brown					X Light
Cream				X	X
Green			X Jade		X Pale
Grey					X
Gold	X		X		
Lavender				X	X
Orange	X	X	X		
Peach				X	X
Pink				X Warm	X Light
Purple	X	X	X		
Red	X	X	X		
Rose			X	X	X
White					X

Color   *Cognitive or Symbolic Impact*

Avoid yellow-green (next to Green row)

Avoid stark whites (next to White row)

Keep in mind the fact that each person will have a different response to color, influenced by his or her experiences. While red might excite many children, it could actually relax the child who associates the color with his or her favorite stuffed animal or "night night" blanket. Color is an accent for instruction.

Learn the New Word...with Color

Objective: Help students learn the alphabet, spelling, and vocabulary using color.

Directions: Bold colors, such as orange, red and shades of lemony yellow demand attention. Reproduce the "learn the word" cards on colored paper, and use black marker to print the words (or letters). You may also use white or cream-colored paper, but select markers in a bold shade to attract the learner's attention. Remember, black and white alone are monotonous.

Just a Stroke of Red (or Orange) for Good Measure

Objective: Research shows that an occasional bold stroke of red or orange attracts the learner's attention to details. Use the following reproducibles to create lessons that ask the learner to identify critical information.

You can use the space below to put text, numbers or symbols for the student to mark. For example, you might print a list of words, ask children to mark the blends (bl, sl, sk) or a list of numbers and ask children to mark out groups of five (5). Photocopy the list and pass it out to your students along with the apple reproducible on page 9, or the orange reproducible on page 10.

_____

_____

_____

_____

_____

_____

_____

_____

_____

_____

Directions for the students: Color the apple red. Red helps you to remember.
Now use your red crayon or pencil to circle every

_____.

Note: Both red and orange are useful for alerting children to specific points of knowledge or new concepts. How can you also incorporate scent or taste in these lessons? See _Differentiated Pathways of the Brain_ (Lorenz Educational Press, 90/1039LE) for ideas.

Name_____   Date _____

Mark in Orange

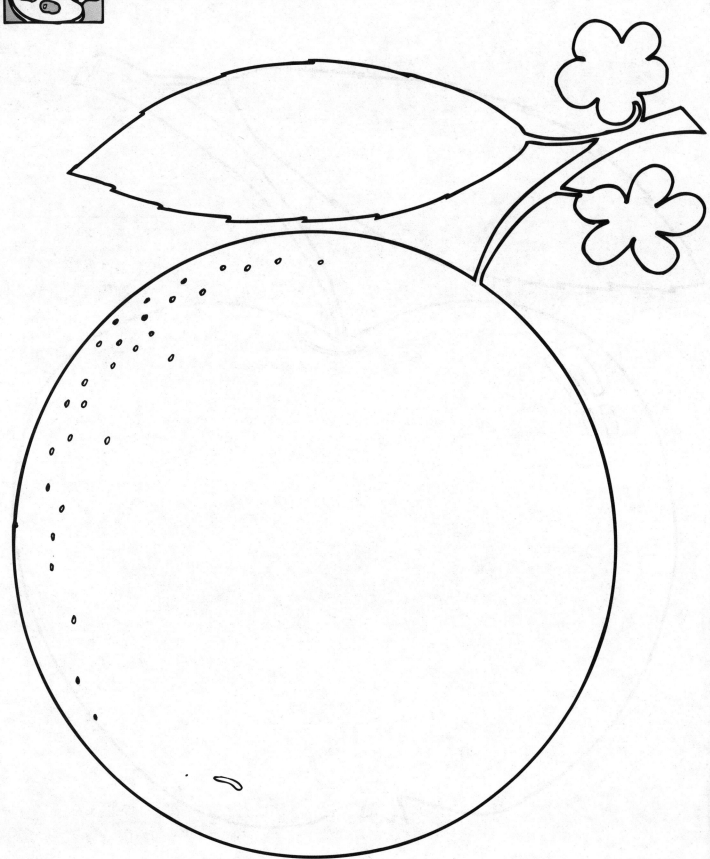

Name_____   Date _____

Color Your World

_____

Your teacher will choose music for you to listen to while you create original artwork.

Listen as the music plays; use your art materials to draw a picture of _____.

Original artwork by _____.

Note: See *Differentiated Pathways of the Brain* (90/1039LE) for specific music recommendations to accompany this activity.

Color for Vocabulary Enrichment

Objective: Color and color words have symbolic and literary value. Use this knowledge to build fluency in oral language.

Directions: You may do this activity aloud or as a written activity for older children. How about creating a class *Big Book of Color Words*? You could have two pages for each color, or more if you want, and then compile them into a booklet, using the cover on page 16.

As green as _____

Name_____ Date _____

Color for Vocabulary Enrichment

As *orange* as _____

As *brown* as _____

Color for Vocabulary Enrichment

As purple as _____

As yellow as _____

Name_____   Date _____

Color for Vocabulary Enrichment

As red as _____

As blue as _____

As Colorful as It Can Be

After children complete the pages for *As Colorful as It Can Be*, create original booklets by using this page as a cover. You might display this and other works on one of the bulletin boards suggested in the following section.

As Colorful as It Can Be

Pages 17-22 contain ideas for sensory-stimulating bulletin boards for your students to create in the classroom. Suggested uses and color themes are included, and reproducible patterns are provided.

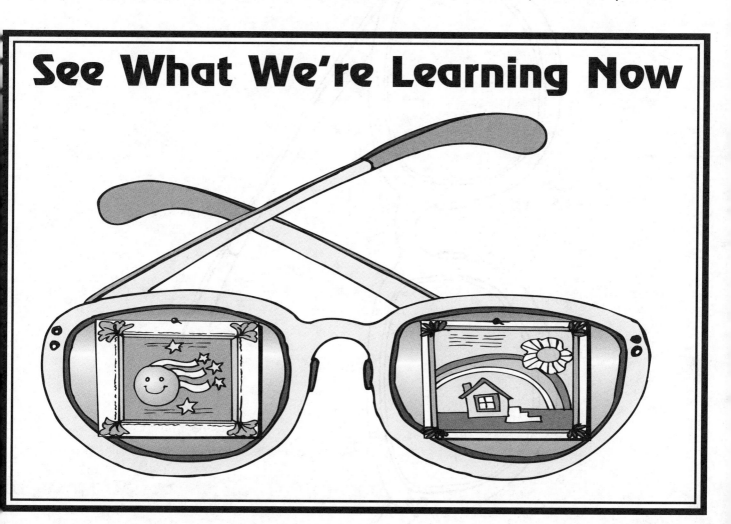

Background Color: yellow or orange

Accent Colors: blue, green, navy

Themes: See What We're Learning Now

Description: Large pair of spectacles cut out of accent colors with examples of student work placed *inside of them.*

Uses: Make this an interactive board. Children put new work up daily and place the other work in their portfolios.

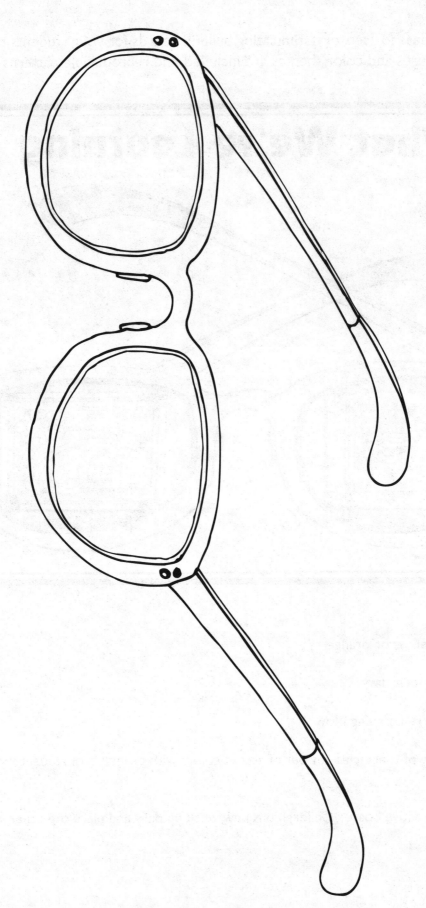

Growing More Creative Every Day

Background Color: jade green, sky blue, warm yellow

Accent Colors: rose and peach

Themes: Growing More Creative Every Day

Description: Intense colored background for flowers and flowerpots that have examples of student work

Uses: creative writing, original artwork, stories, songs, puppets

Try: Use wallpaper samples in bold prints for the flowers, or teach the children to fold tissue paper flowers for a 3-D look.

Light Up the Left Brain with Math

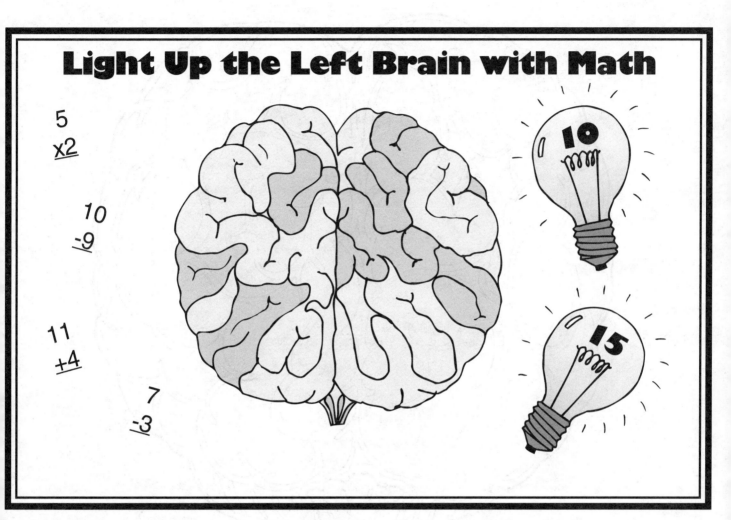

$$\begin{array}{r} 5 \\ \times 2 \\ \hline \end{array}$$

$$\begin{array}{r} 10 \\ -9 \\ \hline \end{array}$$

$$\begin{array}{r} 11 \\ +4 \\ \hline \end{array}$$

$$\begin{array}{r} 7 \\ -3 \\ \hline \end{array}$$

Background Color: light green

Accent Colors: warm brown, yellow, aqua

Themes: Light Up the Left Brain with Math

Description: The left side of the brain is used to process math problems. Make this a practice board for math skills. Each problem is written on the "left side" of the brain. Solutions are written on the light bulbs that are stored in a pocket on the board. Children use wipe-off markers to write a solution on a bulb and then Velcro™ or pin it to the "right side" of the brain.

Uses: For drill and practice of skills in any area of mathematics

Bulletin Board Patterns

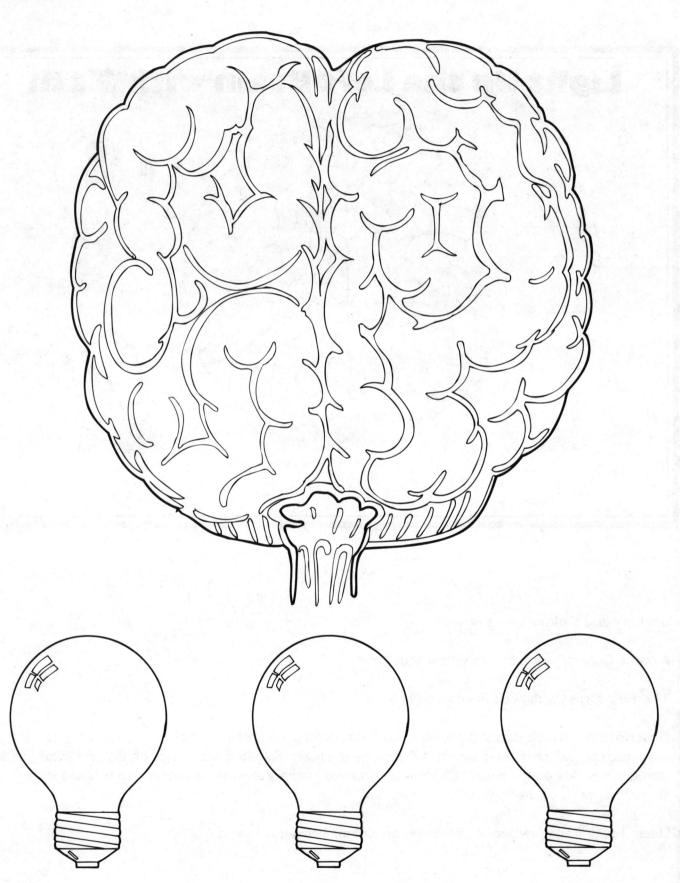

Objective: Children create blue bandages to place under the text or problem that they are working on to help them focus.

Rationale: Some evidence suggests that children who reverse numbers or letters may have a visual tracking problem that produces dyslexia. Of course, any child who displays serious learning problems should be referred for evaluation, both physical and psychological.

Directions: For a classroom bandage, reproduce these "blue bandages" on firm blue or light grey paper. You might also fasten the strips to a craft stick to create an easily held tool. Consider spraying the "blue bandages" with a cinnamon or lemon air freshener to give a sensory boost.

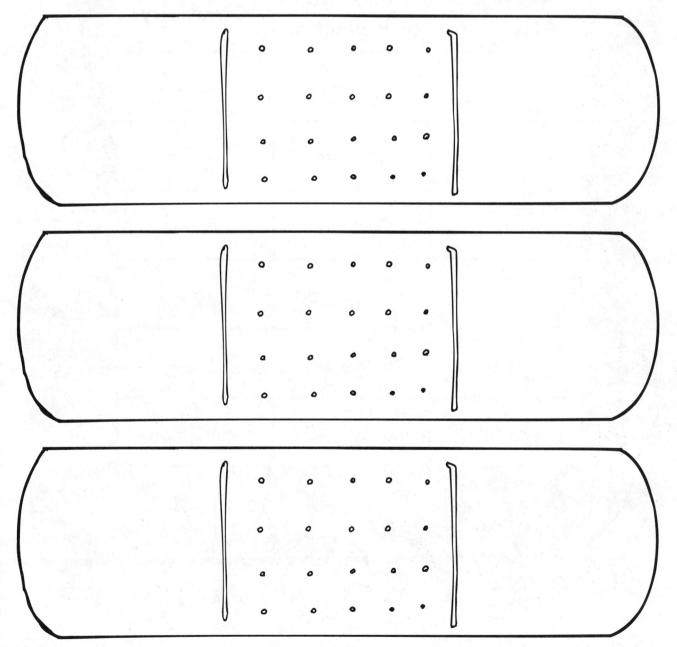

Outcomes

Alertness or Attention	Relaxation or Reflection	Creativity
peppermint	chamomile	sage
wintergreen	jasmine	apple
pine	lavender	rosemary
lemon	sandalwood	rose
eucalyptus	marjoram	basil
spearmint	honeysuckle	cinnamon

Attention-Grabbing Scents

Use the techniques offered in this section by associating the new letters, words or sound blends with pungent scents from the chart on page 24. You can use plain white paper, but be sure to use an attention-grabbing marker color such as yellow, orange or red. If you use a colored paper in a pattern that is designed to match your unit of study (for example, orange pumpkins or green leaves), be sure to use black marker for the best visual appeal.

Note: Reproducible patterns for a lemon (page 28), a pinecone (page 29), and a peppermint (page 31) are included. Write your ideas here for using these attention-grabbing scents to introduce new language skills or to reinforce previously learned skills.

Lemons for Learning Language

Objective: Introduce new letters, sounds or symbols in the classroom using the color and scent of lemons.

Rationale: The scent of lemon seems to promote alertness, and the color yellow seems to have the same effect. Copy the lemon pattern on page 28 on to yellow paper *and* add the scent of lemon to create a favorable situation. Many of these activities can be modified to use the scent of pine, which is also thought to help keep students alert. Reproducible pine cones can be found on page 29.

Directions:

- Print letters on the lemons and have the children trace them with a citrus-scented marker.

- Write new vocabulary words on the lemons and have children glue citrus-flavored cereal circles on the words.

- Write an initial consonant on a lemon and then let the children work in pairs to find pictures in magazines of objects that begin with the sound. These pictures should be glued on another lemon. Staple, glue or string the two lemons together and hang from the ceiling with clear fishing line.

- Use the lemon pattern to make individual glossaries. Children should enter their words in the glossary with a citrus-scented marker or work in an area scented with lemon.

Objective: Use the scent, flavor, and color of lemons to help teach and reinforce mathematical concepts.

Rationale: The scent of lemon seems to promote alert and attentive behavior. This is critical when a child is working with numbers. Use the lemon pattern and the scent of lemon on stickers or with lemon-flavored cereal pieces to reinforce the mathematical concepts of counting, sorting, patterning or one-to-one correspondence.

Directions:

- Cut out smaller (3" [8 cm]) versions of the lemon pattern on page 28, or better still, have the children cut them out for great fine motor practice. Then give each child a plastic bag of 10 "lemons" to use in various counting exercises:
    - Write a number or number word on one of the large lemons and pair up children to count out the appropriate number of smaller lemons.
    - Give oral problem-solving tasks that children can solve by using the lemons. For example: If Juan goes to the market to buy 6 lemons but he drops 2 on the way home, how many lemons will be left to make lemonade?

- The citrus-fresh scent of fruity cereal rings makes them a good manipulative for sorting and patterning. Use the rings to make patterns or to sort into plastic cups. String them on yarn or use them to create a design on paper.

- Mix lemon juice in tempera paint and finger-paint the number words or numbers that you are learning. Use one tablespoon (15 ml) lemon juice per cup of paint. You can also do this with language tasks.

- Give children small cups of lemonade to sip before you work on math tasks. This is refreshing, and the scent and taste will linger as they attend to their work.

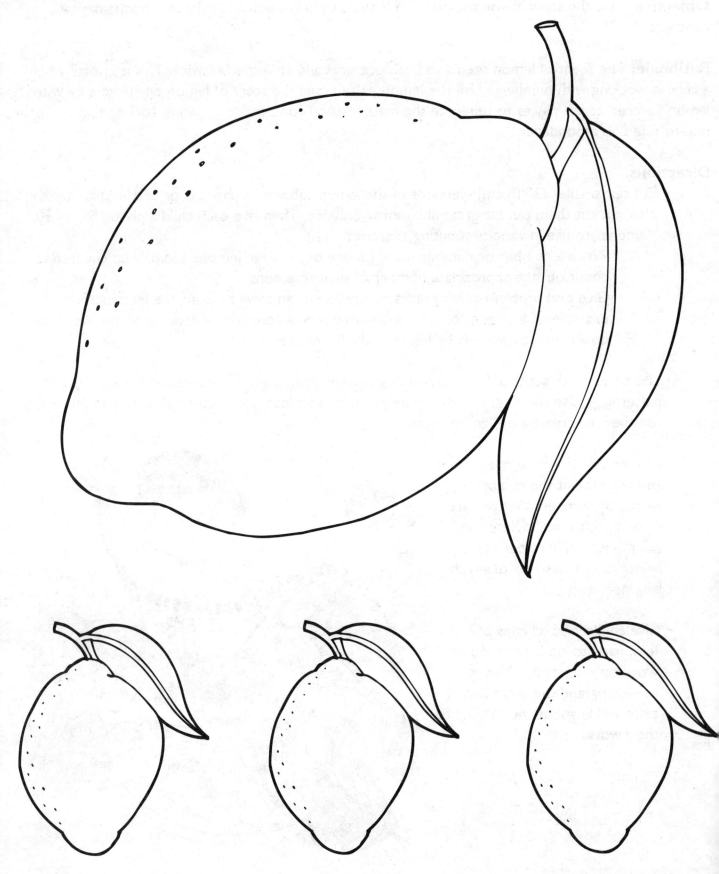

Peppermints for Powerful Learning

Objective: Introduce new concepts, take a quiz or do an assessment.

Rationale: The scent and taste of peppermint seem to "pep up" the brain, making children more alert.

Directions:

- Give the children peppermint or wintergreen-scented markers to highlight words that they have written on a chart story or in their journals.

- Use peppermint candies as math manipulatives to be counted and matched as you teach number concepts.

- Heat the oil of peppermint in a scent pot as you give new instructions or do an assessment.

- Swirl peppermint flavor into milk at snack time to brighten attitudes.

- Offer peppermint lozenges for children to suck on as they learn new letters or sounds. (Not recommended for small children for whom hard candy may pose a choking hazard.)

- The reproducible peppermint candy on page 31 can be used for a writing activity, such as practicing spelling or vocabulary words. Children can cut out the 10 small mints for use as math manipulatives.

Soothing Scents

Children can trace and cut the honeysuckle and lavender patterns and then color them. Decorate the reading center or other quiet areas with homemade vines or restful flowers, sprayed with scent.

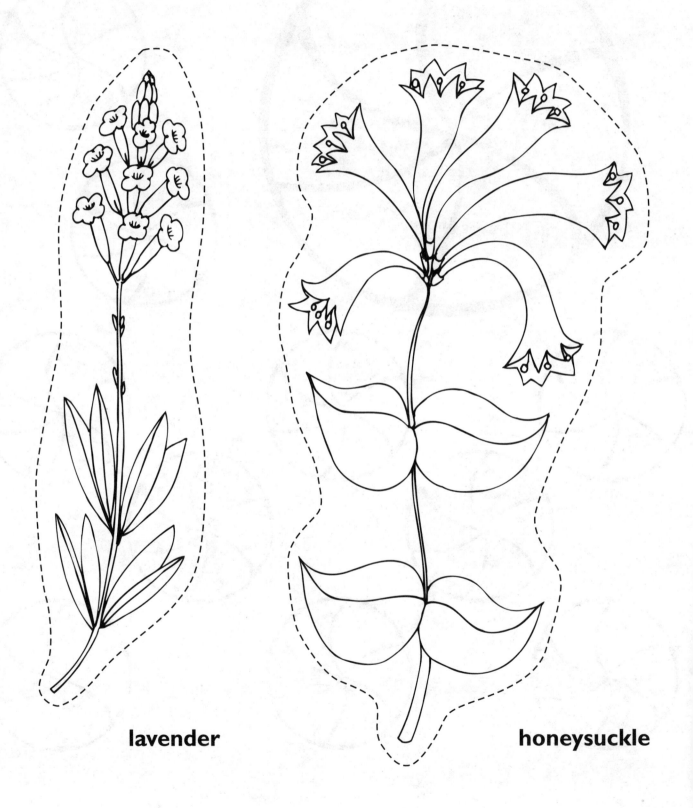

lavender

honeysuckle

"Scent"sational Learning for Creative Times

Use the patterns for the gingerbread man and apple (page 9) whenever you wish to promote a creative flow of ideas in the classroom. Remember, the scent that you spray on these papers or use in the area should enhance creativity. But don't limit your own creativity. Consult the *Color and Cognition Chart* on page 6 to see how these patterns can be colored or reproduced to make full use of a sensory experience.

- Use the patterns for a creative writing exercise.
- Use the patterns as an easel for drawing or painting.
- Use the patterns as postcards to send to pen pals.
- Use the patterns to make original books.
- Use the patterns as mini story boards for math problems.

Rose Pattern

The scent of rose seems to invoke creativity. Reproduce the rose pattern to serve as the pages for individual *A Garden of Thoughts* journals. Children can write poems, stories or ideas in these journals, or share their experiences. Again, consult the *Color and Cognition Chart* on page 6 to make the most "sense" of this idea!

Name_____ Date _____

Spicy Word Scramble

The pungent scent of cinnamon and other spices might help the brain to stay alert or retrieve information from long-term memory. Here's a word scramble that uses spicy words to warm up the brain.

Unscramble the words below.

o m n c n i a n _____

r n g g i e _____

a s l e p l i c _____

r m o m d a a c _____

m n i t _____

g t e m u n _____

o e c v l s _____

c a r l i o t n _____

t m y h e _____

e e r p p p _____

Word Bank

cloves	mint	thyme	pepper	cinnamon
cardamom	ginger	nutmeg	allspice	cilantro

Taste the Learning Chart

Taste or Food Source	Possible Influence on Behavior or Mood
Carbohydrates	Releases endorphins: quiet, tranquil mood. Too much at lunch, and the children will nod off. Save these for afternoon snack time.
Protein	Delivers energy jolt to the system. Feeds the brain. Good for morning snack time.
Vanilla	Calm, reflective mood enhancer
Peppermint	Attention-grabber; may help retrieve information from memory
Ginger or Cinnamon	Calms nausea; enhances creativity
Apple	Natural sweet for energy, with a scent that promotes creativity
Orange	Energy jolt with a color and scent that make a complete "alertness" package
Almond	Enormous protein boost with a scent that is relaxing as well. Good snack for precooperative group lesson.

Apple, Almond, and Raisin Salad

Objective: This activity provides practice in mathematical concepts of estimating and problem solving.

Rationale: The taste, scent, texture and color of this treat deliver a "wake up" call to the brain. It is an excellent morning snack, designed to build up the learning curve during the critical morning hours of instruction. Use the *Problem-Solving Work Area* sheet on page 38 to assess children's performance in this task.

Ingredients:

- sliced red and green apples (skins on)*
- ¼ cup (60 ml) of raisins for each child
- 1 cup (240 ml) of slivered almonds
- 1 tsp. (5 ml) cinnamon or ginger

*You will need one apple for every three children.

Directions: Children should wash their hands and the work table area first. Working in pairs, children mix the ingredients in a large mixing bowl. Children in first grade or higher can also measure all ingredients from the boxes or bags. Sprinkle the mixture with cinnamon or ginger and stir well. Hand out paper cups and challenge the children to figure out how to equally divide the mixture so that every person can try the snack.

Inquiry Questions:

- What should you do first?

- Can you think of any tools that might help you?

- What do we mean by *equal*?

- How can we work together to do this?

- Can you think of a different way to figure this out?

Name_____ Date _____

Problem-Solving Work Area

How much salad do we need? _____

Number of children in the class: _____

Tools I can use to measure or estimate: _____

_____

_____

I estimate that we will need _____ cups of salad. I think this is true, because of

_____

_____

_____

Now I know the answer is _____ because we

_____

_____

_____

"Orange" You Glad It Is Science Time?

Objective: The color, scent and taste of orange make it a natural learning tool. Use this incentive to create an observation on the way that matter changes when temperature is adjusted.

Materials:
- 1 cup (240 ml) of chilled orange juice for each child
- paper cups for drinking
- 3 cups (720 ml) orange juice plus 2 cups (480 ml) ginger ale for freezing
- ice trays with dividers
- toothpicks or craft sticks

Directions: Divide the class into two laboratory teams. Team 1 is responsible for pouring and serving the chilled juice and for handing out copies of the observation sheet on page 40 and orange crayons. Team 2 is responsible for pouring the orange-ginger ale mixture into ice trays and placing them into the freezer.

Assign a timekeeper to set and watch the timer or clock for 45 minutes. At this time, insert toothpicks or craft sticks into the ice trays to serve as skewers.

Print the words *matter*, *solid*, *liquid*, *gas*, *cold* and *freeze* on the board, or better still, on a chart, using a scented orange marker. Discuss these terms prior to the activity time.

Activity:

Step 1: Children sip the cold juice and complete the questions on the observation sheet.

Step 2: Children observe and then eat the frozen juice cubes and then complete the items on the observation sheet.

Name_____ Date _____

"Orange" You Glad It Is Science Time?

Task 1: Describe the cold orange juice.
How did it look and feel?
You can draw a picture or
write your answer here.

Task 2: Was the juice a solid or a liquid? How do you know this?

_____

_____

_____

Task 3: What happened to the juice after it went into the freezer?

_____

_____

_____

Task 4: Describe the juice after it was frozen. You can draw it, too.

_____

_____

Using words from the vocabulary list and pictures that you draw, tell what you know about how things change when they are frozen. Why?

_____

_____

Quiet Time Cereal Snack: A High Carbohydrate Relaxer

Objective: Use this snack as a prelude to reading a story aloud to the children.

Rationale: The subtle flavors, texture, chewing and nutrients will relax them. See the suggestions for color and scent on pages 6 and 24 for use in read-aloud areas.

Materials:
- 2 cups (480 ml) of oat rings
- 2 cups of puffed rice
- 2 cups of wheat squares
- 2 cups of corn squares
- 2 cups of fruit-filled cereal squares
- 2 cups of corn puffs
- $^2/_3$ cup chopped almond pieces
- $^2/_3$ cup dark chocolate morsels
- $^2/_3$ cup raisins or chopped dates

*None of the cereals should have added sugar or frosting. Use generic store brands for a wholesome but less expensive cereal. Avoid peanuts because of the incidence of allergies.

Directions: Children should mix this snack in a large sealable, plastic bag. Mix together all of the whole grain cereals and add the remaining ingredients. Shake well. The snack should be served in white paper cups that the children have decorated with scenes from "what they think the story will be about." Share the title of the book, then pass out markers and crayons. While the "helpers" mix the snack, others can design their cups.

Extension: Extend this activity by using the *Reading Reflection Page* (page 42) after reading the story aloud.

Name_____ Date _____

Reading Reflection Page

The name of the story is _____.

The author of the story is _____.

An illustrator named _____ drew the art for this story.

This is a good story because

_____

_____

_____

Here is a picture about the story.

Two words that describe this story are _____ and

_____.

Objective: Reinforce geometric concepts using slices of cheese.

Rationale: Slices of yellow cheese provide a colorful incentive for the senses. The protein lift is critical to learning.

Materials:
- cookie cutters in geometric shapes (spray with non-stick vegetable cooking spray first)
- two slices of cheese per child (four shapes)
- crackers in geometric shapes
- waxed paper

Directions: Spread the work area with waxed paper. Place cookie cutters in circle, square, diamond, triangle, rectangle and oval shapes in a basket or margarine tub. Children should wash their hands and then use the cookie cutters to practice cutting slices of cheese with the cutters. Children can match the cheese shapes to crackers that have the same shape.

Extension: After snacking on the high protein cheese, use the *Cut and Paste Shape Page* (page 44) to reinforce the names and designs of shapes. What colors could also help reinforce this lesson? Refer to page 6.

Cut and Paste Shape Page

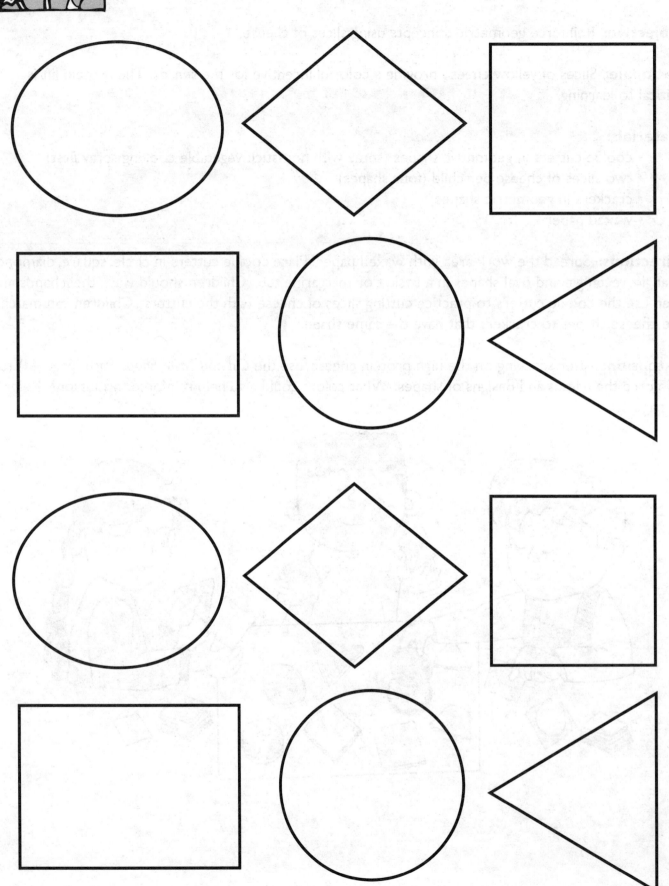

44

Taste-Based Activities

Creative Snacking: Carrot, Celery, and Peanut Butter Creatures

Objective: Students use their creativity to build a creature using healthy snacks.

Rationale: Fresh vegetables and peanut butter offer an energy lift by sending protein to the brain and vitamins A and C to the nervous system. The bold colors of carrots and celery also enhance attention.

Materials:

- margarine tubs filled with ice water
- carrot sticks
- celery sticks
- plastic knives or craft sticks for spreading
- plastic cups of peanut butter
- assorted toppings: raisins, peanuts, coconut, pickle chunks, pineapple pieces, carob chips
- margarine tub lids for sitting the creatures on

Directions: Place the carrot and celery sticks in the ice water to harden. Working in small groups of four to six at a time, the children are encouraged to design original snack creatures. Remember to wash hands first and to teach the importance of eating what you use. Waste not; want not!

Extension: After completing the creatures, extend this lesson to writing and art by using the *Picture My Creature* and *Creature Verse* reproducible on page 46.

Name_____ Date _____

Picture My Creature

Draw your creature...

Write about your creature...

Creature Verse

A celery and carrot _____, that is what I made.

It is bigger than a _____.

I am not afraid!

With arms like _____, and a tail of power.

You will eat up my _____ in less than one hour!

Listen and Snack...A Fun Way to Follow Directions

Objective: Students will practice following oral directions.

Rationale: Vanilla is a relaxing flavor, so vanilla frosting is used in this activity.

Ingredients:
- one tub of vanilla frosting
- plastic knives or craft sticks for spreading
- graham crackers (one large cracker per child)
- red cinnamon candies
- pretzel sticks (two per child)

Directions: This activity is best completed in small groups of four to six children at a time. Prepare the work area by spreading waxed paper on the table and setting out ingredients in baskets or on a tray.

Read the directions aloud:
1. Take one graham cracker and place it in front of you.
2. Using a plastic knife or craft stick, cut the cracker in fourths (demonstrate). You will have four rectangles.
3. Spread pieces with vanilla frosting.
4. Place one cracker piece in front of you. This will be the head of your animal.
5. Use pretzel sticks to make antlers on your animal.
6. Use cinnamon candies to make the nose, eyes and mouth.
7. What animal did you make? (deer or reindeer)

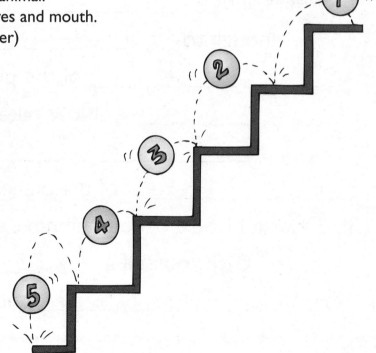

Anytime Following Directions Snack Story

Objective: Students will learn to follow oral directions.

Directions: Choose a high protein, colorful snack treat that can be easily picked up and eaten or manipulated as part of the story. Pass the snack out to the students.

Fill in the blanks below to create your own story. Students will use their snack pieces to follow the directions you have written. Improvise and use this sheet often.

Choose _____ of the

_____ and place them on your

_____. Now _____

with _____ of the pieces. How many are left? Take

those pieces, and put them in order from _____

to _____. Now take _____ more

pieces and _____ with them. Do you have

enough to _____? Now you may eat

_____ of the pieces. With the rest, try to

_____. Now, take a piece of paper and draw

_____. Put

_____ of the pieces of _____ in

it. Draw a picture of yourself next to the _____.

Give yourself a _____ and a

_____ and a big, hungry mouth.

You may finish eating the snack. Good listening.

Name_____   Date _____

Recipe Card to Send Home

From the Classroom of _____

Chef: _____

We made: _____

You will need: _____

_____

_____

_____

_____

You will do: _____

_____

_____

_____

_____

_____

Don't forget to: _____

_____

_____

_____

Clean-Shave for Smooth Thinking

Objective: Use shaving cream to reinforce language, math, science, and other concepts.

Rationale: Shaving cream offers an inexpensive yet stimulating medium for enhancing learning and creativity. Choose the menthol or mint scents to further entice the senses and cognition.

Materials:
- shaving cream
- waxed paper or other material to cover the "writing" surface

Directions: Spray a thick layer of chilled shaving cream on waxed paper or on an old shower curtain (floor), or on a picnic tabletop (outdoors) that has been covered with newspaper. Use it to:

- Illustrate the blending of colors or to practice making color families by mixing food coloring drops into the cream.
- Imprint objects, such as shells, leaves, or rocks to make "instant fossils" and to help learn the names of new objects by making a tactile connection.
- Draw "pictures" in the snow to go along with a unit on winter or seasons.
- Practice writing names. This is good for both print or cursive letters.
- Work in pairs to spell and check the weekly vocabulary words or spelling list.
- Solve number problems in the cream and check them with a calculator.
- Use cookie cutters to imprint geometric shapes and then learn the names.

Your idea: _____

_____

_____

Your idea: _____

_____

_____

Your idea: _____

_____

_____

Rebus Stories with a New Twist

Objective: Students will create rebus stories using sensory-rich stickers.

Rationale: The rebus story has long been an effective teaching tool. One simply inserts a picture to represent a word. But with so many kinds of stickers on the market, especially fuzzy, furry, glitter, neon or scented stickers, the opportunity for high-touch learning becomes huge!

Directions: Use the reproducible on page 52 to create original rebus stories. Be sure to provide a wide variety of stickers that go along with the theme or unit.

Hints:

- Keep the stickers in folders or sealed margarine tubs, organized by themes: animal stickers, nature stickers, people stickers, planet stickers.
- Use recycled file folders, cut into one-half pieces, to "mount" your pages.
- See pages 6 and 24 for ideas for using color and scent as the children create rebus stories or books.
- Place the rebus books on one of the display boards described on pages 17 to 22.
- Put the rebus books into a creative arts portfolio cover.
- Give the children adequate time to create something like this. It cannot be rushed.
- Always review vocabulary words before beginning such an activity.
- Encourage children to share their rebus stories, either with a partner, parent volunteer or with a teacher. Creativity needs open, lavish *encouragement!*

Rebus Story Patterns

Objective: Use the mosaic technique to create a pattern or design picture.

Rationale: Mosaic technique involves cutting, shredding, tearing or punching out a cloth or paper material that will then be used to create a picture. Mosaic is high touch but also draws on color and texture to make a rich learning and creative encounter.

Directions: Provide materials for the mosaic and a sturdy background on which to create the mosaic. Show children a few examples to help them bridge over to this new experience. Use the *Mosaic Matrix* below to help stimulate your own creative ideas.

Possible Materials	Methods	Adhesives	Possible Backgrounds
tissue paper	punch	colored glue	recycled file folders
wallpaper sample or old greeting cards	tear	white glue	construction paper
construction paper	cut	paste	wood
felt pieces	trace shapes	craft glue	wallpaper samples
wrapping paper	strips	clear glue	fabric

Note: The matrix is meant to be used openly. Skip around and choose one from each list. They are not in a special order. Be creative.

Holiday Hands-On Brain Craft

Objective: Students will create a simple gift that could help parents curb the effects of stress during the busy holiday season.

Rationale: Can you imagine a more welcome holiday treat than one that might actually help to make children more alert during the learning process or more reflective during the creative process? Read on to discover a fun-to-make "Brain Treat" that doubles as a holiday craft for children and to find important information about how the brain works.

Materials:
- Clean, recycled large jelly or canning jars with lids
- Bags of wrapped mints, cinnamon disks, root beer barrels, and butterscotch disks
- Decorating materials for the lids: Small scented pinecones and colored calico "skirts" can be effective.
- Large self-sticking labels on which to print the accompanying poem

Directions:
1. Layer clean glass jars with 2 inches of candy. It works best with a distinct layer of colors. For example: red and white mints, followed by butterscotch, followed by green and white mints, followed by root beer barrels.
2. Print out the poem on the labels and apply to the front of each jar.
3. Decorate the lids with holiday ribbons, raffia, yarn, buttons, or even small pinecones with glitter. The scent of pine is a stress reducer!
4. Screw the lids onto the jars after the glue has dried.

The Poem: Your labels will convey the brain-friendly message explaining why this is no ordinary jar of candy!

A Holiday Brain Treat for You
Peppermint and wintergreen
Can soothe away where stress has been.
Refreshing scents to calm the brain
And make you want to think again.
Smell the charm of ginger and spice.
Your brain thinks this is very nice!
Cinnamon to ease the fray.
Butterscotch to calm the day.
Colors like red to energize,
Calming green to fertilize.
A mind too tired from holiday stress
Needs nature's palette to give it rest.
Warm colors and scents lend creative spark,
A light for the mind in the wintery dark.
So reach in your hand and pull out a treat-
Minty or spicy, tangy or sweet.

Beach Balls on the Brain

Just when you thought that there couldn't possibly be anything new in your teaching repertoire, re-think the old vinyl beach ball. Inexpensive enough to purchase a dozen to outfit for different fields of inquiry, the beach ball teaching tool is a great way to jazz up instruction.

Not only is the beach ball teaching tool fun, it helps to stimulate neurons. Like any other physical structure, the brain stays flexible when it is used often and with a full measure of energy. Teachers can use simple props such as a vinyl, inflatable beach ball to keep neurons zipping about the pre-frontal cortex. How can this be accomplished? Think of using the beach ball prop in five ways:

• **As a stimulating technique.** Toss the beach ball to students to catch as a way of involving them in a discussion. Pass the beach ball around a circle of chairs to keep energy and momentum going. Move the beach ball around a room in time to music to activate the auditory modality of learning.

• **As a tool of inquiry.** This is one of my favorite methods. Using an inexpensive, inflatable beach ball and a permanent marker, write questions or prompts on each colored stripe. Toss or pass the ball to a student and invite him or her to respond to the question or prompt that "lands" facing him or her. I have designed several "themes" to use on different beach balls so that teachers can vary the routine. These prompts and questions appear in boxes on page 56.

• **As a classroom management tool.** Print the names of group members on the stripes of balls and keep the collection of balls in a colorful child's wading pool in your activity area. This adds a sense of fun to any day. Pull out a ball and flip it around until you come to a child's name and use it to 1) Grab attention; 2) Ask a question; or 3) Allow a child to ask a question. Use it to review for a test. Start by tossing it to "Jamal" whose name is on the yellow stripe. When he answers correctly, allow him to toss it to the next child who will answer the review question.

• **As a mini-therapy ball.** Using the same method described above, inscribe the stripes of the ball with prompts from the affective, rather than cognitive domain of learning. Giving voice to one's feelings, positive or negative, is a good way to keep serotonin levels even in the brain. This optimizes brain function. We also know that children's thinking skills are impaired while they are under stress, so a beach ball activity can be therapeutic. Appropriate prompts appear below:

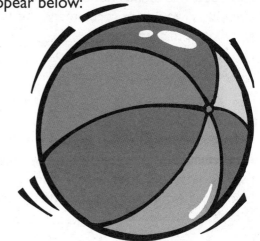

• Today, I feel like_____.
• I am happy today because_____.
• I am feeling worried today because_____.
• Something is on my mind today and it is_____.
• I would like to talk about _____.
• Something that gives me joy is_____.
• I feel good when I think of_____.

• **As a physical activity tool.** The brain works best when plenty of oxygen is flowing. Even simple physical activities can increase oxygen flow with amazing results. Using music if you like and a variety of simple props, give beach balls to each participant or to pairs of students and try the following prompts:

- Lift the ball over your head.
- Pass the ball to your partner.
- Toss the ball into the laundry basket.
- Squeeze the ball with both hands.
- Roll the ball to your partner
- Hold the ball in your arms and move them side to side.
- Touch your nose with the ball.
- Roll the ball under the table.

This is a nice way to transition from a stressful activity to a more low key one, or to help students focus their attention. A simple beach ball can go a long way in livening up an activity session. Try using "beach music" from a CD. It is time to nudge some neurons into action! Create themed beach balls to match your classroom needs.

Theme #1
Learning
* What do you remember about _____ ?
* Can you name something new that we did today?
* What is the name of _____ ?
* Can you tell me something new about _____ ?
* What is the word that means _____ ?

Theme #2
Connections
* How did _____ and _____ go together?
* Did you ever do this before?
* What does _____ remind you of?
* When was the last time we _____ ?
* This is something that my friend _____ would like.

Theme #3
Book or Story Ball Activity
* I thought the main character was _____ .
* This book was or was not entertaining.
* I would or would not recommend this book to a friend.
* The plot of this story was _____ .
* The author's style reminds me of _____ .

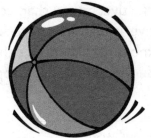

Theme #4
Evaluation Ball
* I rate today's activity a _____ on a scale of 1 to 5.
* This activity was definitely worth my time. Yes or No?
* I would or would not like to try this again.
* I would or would not recommend this to a friend.
* Today's activity left me feeling _____ .

Theme #5
Social Studies
* Go to the globe and find _____ .
* Go to the map and find _____ .
* What is the capital of _____ ?
* Which country or state borders _____ ?
* Name 3 facts about _____ .

Listen to Nature

Objective: Use this experience to reinforce one or more of these skills: listening, auditory discrimination, verbal fluency, auditory memory, creative thinking, problem solving, and small motor skills (drawing, cutting, and pasting).

Rationale: Soothing, yet stimulating recordings of "natural things" can stimulate children's imaginations or prompt memories of pleasant outdoor experiences.

Directions: After reading a story that contains scenes or characters from nature (whales, swamps, birds, meadows), lower the lights and ask the children to listen quietly as you play a recording of one of the following:

- sounds of the swamp
- whale songs
- sounds of the meadow
- bird songs
- ocean sounds

After listening to the nature recording, have students work with a partner or small group to make a list of all the sounds that they heard. Then have them draw a picture of what they think the scene looked like.

Do You Hear What I Hear?

Objective: Students will practice their auditory discrimination and auditory memory skills.

Directions: Make a list of words or pictures of sounds that can be heard in the nature recording, making sure to omit one of the more dominant sounds. Add several extra words or pictures to this list of sounds that were not heard in the recording. Transfer this list to the top box on the *Do You Hear What I Hear?* activity sheet on page 60. Reproduce and pass out the sheet to the students, and play the nature recording.

Name_____ Date _____

Listen to Nature

This is what we heard in the _____.

_____   _____

_____   _____

_____   _____

_____   _____

This is what I think it looks like in the _____.

Do You Hear What I Hear?

Directions: After listening to a nature recording, look at the list of words or pictures below. If you hear this sound, circle the item in green. If you did not hear this sound, circle the item in red.

We left an important sound out...can you draw a picture of it?

Sound-Based Activities

Cutter

Finder of Pictures

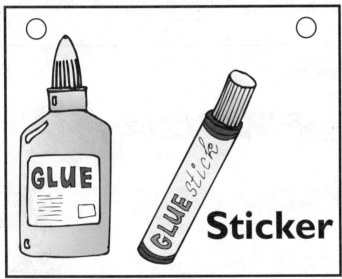

Sticker

Time Keeper

Materials: Nature magazines, travel brochures, catalogs, safety scissors, paste, tagboard

Directions: After listening to the nature sounds recording, look through old magazines and cut out pictures of the animals, grass, water or sky that you "heard" in the picture. Imagine what the scene looked like, and then create a collage using the pictures and paste. A collage is many little pictures glued together. Try not to have any white space on your paper. Fill it with color!

Working in a group is an important skill. Use the nametags above for this and other cooperative group activities. Laminate and punch holes to make a necklace.

Objective: Students will practice verbal fluency by recording their conversations.

Directions: After listening to the nature recording, students may have a lot of interesting ideas about what was going on. What animal sounds did they hear? Was there water? Do the students think it was warm or cool in the place? Use a tape recorder and blank tape or digital recording system to record their ideas. Have students tell a story about what they heard.

Provide a tape player and blank tapes or set up an alternative recording system. Use the checklist below if you wish to place an evaluation of this activity in the child's speech and language portfolio. Be sure to date and label the class tapes.

- -

Language Checkpoint

Child: _____ Date: _____

Activity Description: _____

_____

Evaluator: _____ School: _____

Skill	Strength	Competent	Needs Improvement
Length of Sentences			
Syntax and Grammar			
Description/ Creative Use of Language			
Articulation			

Introduction to Gender-Based Learning

When I was invited by Principal Wanda Carroll-Williams to facilitate a single-gender "Inquiry Group" at her school, the charge was simple: to engage teachers in a pilot program for single-gender grouping in ways to "break brain barriers." We were to consider research, practice, and the scenes playing out in the classroom. What seemed to work with boys? Which strategies seemed to engage girls? Where were the connecting points? What followed was a fascinating series of discussions about how and why single gender classrooms operate. Our work together proved so fruitful that we created an article titled, "A Singularly Different Way to Teach and Learn: Teachers' Reports on a Single Gender Choice Model in Grades 2-5 in a Southern, High-Poverty School." In the article, we analyzed test results of students in grades 2-5 who had been placed in single-gender classes for the year and compared their results to students in mixed groupings at both the school and national levels. The results are compelling. Single-gender practices do seem to affect learning in positive ways, if teachers are trained and motivated.

Teachers in this study used the techniques from both *Differentiated Pathways of the Brain* and *Breaking Brain Barriers* during their pilot year, because I was writing the books at the same time. You will have the luxury of trying out fresh ideas that have been field tested by teachers working in a high-poverty school, without a lot of extra money or resources, just like many of you. For the most part, we found that single-gender strategies:

- Are really about style, not substance
- Work best when one dismisses stereotypes and focuses on individuals
- Are closely linked to boys' and girls' natural instincts, including competition, collaboration, and connections
- Allow boys and girls to focus on their learning without the distractions of the opposite sex, which was particularly important in grades 4-5, where we saw the most significant results
- Offer teachers more flexibility to adjust pacing, group sizes, and management styles to accommodate some bold differences among boys and girls

Whether you believe in or have the opportunity to teach in a pure, single-gender setting, even for part of the day or year, consider infusing some of the strategies into your own heterogeneously grouped setting. You may be rather surprised at how boys respond to fractions when they are placed into a "competition" to find the lowest common denominator, or girls spend more time in the block center in kindergarten when one adds props and keeps boys "out" while the girls engage in lengthy, collaborative building projects. As one veteran teacher noted, the boys seemed much more comfortable and fluid in their language while exploring the theme of a powerful novel about the Dust Bowl when she taught them in a single-gender setting. Their written passages were longer and used emotive language. In one of our inquiry sessions, she noted, "It was like they were *free* to be emotional." That's an interesting observation. What might you find as you explore gender-friendly strategies in your own setting?

Sentence Stringing

Objective: To increase language fluency in boys and girls, students will create long, creative sentences using vocabulary words drawn from the chapter, unit or theme under study. The sentences will be constructed using tactile-kinesthetic activity.

Materials:
- noun and verb shapes
- dictionaries
- thesauri
- colored, scented markers
- lists of vocabulary words
- lengths of string or yarn
- hole punch
- scissors

Directions: Students may work in teams, preferably teams containing one boy and one girl. This makes "gender sense" because the boys will have an opportunity for "handling" words by cutting, drawing and stringing, while girls can draw on their more typical fluidity in using language.

1. Begin with a whole group brainstorm session to create a list of words to correlate with the unit under study. On page 66, you will find a sample list for the unit on plants.
2. Post the list on chart paper using colored, scented markers or on an overhead using red or orange pen.
3. Using the appropriate noun and verb shapes (square and circle), the students will construct sentences that use the words correctly. Depending on the developmental level of the students, additional shapes for articles, adjectives, adverbs and prepositions can be added. With younger children, it is best just to use one shape for any kind of word.
4. Team members write one word on each shape and then cut the shapes out and string them, in order, on the sentence string. The words can be attached to the string by punching a hole in the shape (at the top) and securing it to the string with a paper clip, brad or a smaller length of string.
5. Each team will have 10 minutes to construct their sentences. The goal is to create long, robust sentences that make sense.

Assessment Checklist:

The team's sentence contained at least three vocabulary words. _____

The sentence had a subject and verb. _____

The sentence "makes sense." _____

Sentence Stringing Begins with Words

List vocabulary words and other supporting terms here.

_____   _____

_____   _____

_____   _____

_____   _____

_____   _____

_____   _____

_____   _____

_____   _____

_____   _____

_____   _____

_____   _____

_____   _____

_____   _____

Reproducible Shapes

Reproduce these shapes on construction paper.

65 Gender-Based Activities

Sample Sentence Stringing Word List

List vocabulary words and other supporting terms here.

Theme: plants
Grade level: Second to third grade

plants	growing
leaves	sun
Earth	bulbs
photosynthesis	greenhouse
nature	roots
tilling	water
sunshine	stem
flowers	living
pollen	planting
green	needs
soil	seeds
garden	oxygen
seasons	dirt

Recorded Spelling Assessment

More Fluency Builders for Boys and Girls

Objective: Students will use the auditory modality to improve spelling and listening skills.

Materials:
- tape recorder and blank tapes, or digital recording system
- lists of spelling words
- wipe-off boards
- colored markers for rechecks

Directions: Teams (ideally a boy and a girl) will take practice spelling tests using the tape recorder. After studying the spelling or vocabulary words, the teams will pair off and record. One child calls out the words, one at a time, and the other child tapes his or her attempt. Together, the children listen back to the recorded result and rewrite errors on the wipe-off board. Then the children switch places. This activity makes "gender sense" because boys may demonstrate less acute hearing, especially of subtle vowel and consonant sounds, and may also demonstrate difficulty in articulation during the early school years. Practice in listening and taping might strengthen those areas. In addition, use of the visual modality (wipe-off boards) and tactile-kinesthetic act (markers) of recording the errors can help girls strengthen that modality of learning. The sound of one's voice is a self-esteem boost for all children.

Assessment: Save recorded spelling practices and label the tapes with the date of the session and the child's name. Place these tapes in the student's language arts portfolio. Use the following checklist to evaluate any kind of recorded material in the portfolio.

Checklist for Recorded Products

Student: _____ Assessment Date: _____

Number of products under review: _____

Subject Areas: _____

Teacher: _____

	Strength............ Weakness
Skill	4 3 2 1

Articulation
- ○ Consonants _____
- ○ Vowels _____
- ○ Stuttering or slurring _____
- ○ Reversals _____

Pronunciation
- ○ Says words correctly _____
- ○ Dialect interferes _____

Sentence Structure
- ○ Speaks in complete sentences _____
- ○ Uses parts of speech correctly _____
- ○ Seems to understand how
  sentences are formed _____

Language Fluency
- ○ Demonstrates rich vocabulary _____
- ○ Creativity in language _____
- ○ Ease with language _____
- ○ Uses words from both home
  and school _____

Objective: Students will use language to communicate with parents about what is happening at school.

Materials:
- reproducible *Postcards to Parents* cards (page 70)
- pencils

Directions: Each week, students will write a postcard to their parents, completing the prompts about the things they learned or experienced in school that week. This makes "gender sense" because girls often enjoy using language to connect with others, while boys may need practice at articulating what they have experienced.

Note: There are two levels of postcards to choose from. One is for primary children and one is for older students.

Primary Postcard

To:

_____

_____

_____

_____

Elementary/Middle Grade Postcard

To:

_____

_____

_____

_____

Speak Up! I Can't Hear You

Objective: Students will have the opportunity to speak for three minutes about a topic. The other students will practice listening skills and giving feedback.

Rationale: In her book, *You Just Don't Understand: Men, Women and Conversation*, Dr. Deborah Tannen reports that from an early age, girls begin withdrawing verbally in public, afraid to appear too self-assured and smart in front of boys. Boys, on the other hand, begin interrupting girls during conversation, and girls allow it. While this sociological-cultural shaping is going on, one might think that boys have the verbal advantage, but think again. When Dr. Tannen looked at videotapes of boys and girls (separately) who had been instructed to interview one another about a "serious event," the boys showed a distinct disadvantage. Dr. Tannen said, "Comparing the boys and girls of the same age, I had the feeling I was looking at two different species." The boys turned the activity into a rough and tumble game, jumping from topic to topic and not taking the task too seriously. The girls, on the other hand, infused a rich dialogue with empathy and examples from real life. They got into the interviewing task.

We have a curious dichotomy here. Boys may not seem very skilled at dialogue or interview, but in just a few years, they will be taken more seriously than the girls who obviously have a lot to say.

Materials:
> • *My Three Minutes on Stage* sheets (page 72)
> • *Feedback Sheet for "Speak Up!"* worksheets (page 73)

Directions: Offer boys and girls opportunities to plan and execute a short talk early on and also practice listening and giving feedback to one another. This will build skills and, hopefully, respect.

Today's Speaker
Tommy Leone

Name_____ Date _____

My Three Minutes on Stage

Date: _____

Topic: _____

Opening Sentence: _____

_____

_____

_____

_____

Key Ideas: _____

_____

_____

_____

_____

_____

_____

Conclusion: _____

_____

_____

_____

Feedback Sheet for "Speak Up!"

Speaker:_____

1. The speaker kept my attention.   Yes   No

   Comments:_____

   _____

   _____

2. The speaker spoke clearly and could easily be understood.   Yes   No

   Comments:_____

   _____

   _____

3. The talk was organized and easy to follow.   Yes   No

   Comments:_____

   _____

   _____

4. I learned something new or interesting from this talk.   Yes   No

   Comments:_____

   _____

   _____

The Content Interview
Using Language Effectively

Objective: Students will use interviewing techniques to apply content from science, social studies or a piece of literature under study.

Rationale: Research on gender differences in thinking indicate that girls may pay attention to specific content, especially in science, if they recognize its application to their future. In addition, research on boys' use of language suggests that they make everything a game and might respond more enthusiastically with a "let's play interview" technique. In both cases, the content takes on richness as students handle it using higher-order thinking questions found in an interview format.

Materials:
- *Interview the Expert* worksheets (pages 75-76)
- textbooks, study notes, or classroom novels

Directions: There are two reproducible pages for teachers to choose from. One is a blank format on which to transcribe specific content questions. The other is open-ended and generic, for students to use with any topic or book. Have students fill in the appropriate page for the lesson.

Name_____ Date _____

Interview the Expert

Student being interviewed:_____

Interviewer: _____

Topic: _____ Date:_____

Question 1: _____

Response: _____

_____

Question 2: _____

Response: _____

_____

Question 3: _____

Response: _____

_____

Question 4: _____

Response: _____

_____

Question 5: _____

Response: _____

_____

Interview the Expert

Student being interviewed:_____

Interviewer: _____

Topic: _____ Date: _____

Question 1: Can you tell me three important facts about this subject?

Response: _____

_____

_____

Question 2: Explain how you would use something that you learned in this
study to deal with a real-life situation?

Response: _____

_____

Question 3: Can you give the name of an important character, leader or
key person in this study and tell what his or her contribution was?

Response: _____

_____

Question 4: Based on what you have learned, tell me something that is not
true about the subject, something that you might have believed
before, but know better now.

Response: _____

_____

Objective: Students will create trading cards containing information about character, plot, themes and settings in books that they read for pleasure or for class projects.

Rationale: Between the ages of 8 and 12, both boys and girls enjoy collecting sets of just about anything. Collecting builds critical skills such as observation, classification and analysis. This activity makes "gender sense" because boys seem to like making games out of lessons, and girls enjoy telling stories and sharing gossip. The trading card idea taps into boys' interest in sports trading cards and girls' interest in talking about people. Some might find these descriptors as "sexist," but observation of children shows that such gender-specific likes and dislikes are in place by the age of three. Classroom teachers can take advantage of this information to design meaningful activities.

Materials:
- *Trading Cards* reproducible cut-outs (page 78)
- books or novels

Directions:

1. Select the novel or book to be used in preparing the trading cards, and read the book as a class project. A list of high-interest books, by grade level, that appeal to both boys and girls is included (page 79). This list is not meant to be exclusive!

2. Discuss the story as a whole group.

3. Review the concepts of character, plot, setting, conflict and theme.

4. Use the *Trading Cards* reproducible as a template for creating assessments or reviews of the book.

5. Consider a Trading Card Swap with another class. The invitation and ideas follow (page 80).

Trading Card for

_____

Title: _____

Author: _____

The main character is

_____ .

Three words to describe

_____ are: _____ ,

_____ , _____ .

Trading Card for

_____

Title: _____

Author: _____

The main character is

_____ .

Three words to describe

_____ are: _____ ,

_____ , _____ .

Trading Card for

_____

Title: _____

Author: _____

The main character is

_____ .

Three words to describe

_____ are: _____ ,

_____ , _____ .

Trading Card for

_____

Title: _____

Author: _____

The main character is

_____ .

Three words to describe

_____ are: _____ ,

_____ , _____ .

Suggested Books for Trading Cards

2nd Grade

Miss Rumphious by Barbara Cooney

A Sweet, Sweet Basket by Margie Willis Clary

Amazing Grace by Mary Hoffman

Henry and Beezus by Beverly Cleary

Babe: The Story of a Pig by Dick King-Smith

When I Was Young and In the Mountains
    by Cynthia Rylant

Sheila Rae, the Brave by Kevin Henkes

Thank You, Mr. Faulker by Patricia Polacco

3rd Grade

Charlotte's Web by E.B. White

The House at Pooh Corner by A.A. Milne

Bunnicula by Deborah and James Howe

Tuck Everlasting by Natalie Babbitt

The Courage of Sarah Noble by Alice Dalgliesh

Frindle by Andrew Clements

Alfredito Flies Home by Jorge Argueta

4th Grade

First Apple by Ching Yeung Russell

Shiloh by Phyllis Reynolds Naylor

Matilda by Roald Dahl

From the Mixed-Up Files of Mrs. Basil E. Frankweiler
    by E.L. Konigsburg

Holes by Louis Sachar

The Phantom Tollbooth by Norton Juster

Sarah, Plain and Tall by Patricia McLachlan

5th Grade

Black Beauty by Anna Sewell

The Lion, the Witch and the Wardrobe
    by C.S. Lewis

Rascal by Sterling North

Number the Stars by Lois Lowry

Hatchet by Gary Paulsen

Maniac Magee by Jerry Spinelli

Because of Winn-Dixie by Kate DiCamillo

Walk Two Moons by Sharon Creech

Middle School

Island of the Blue Dolphins or The Black Pearl
    by Scott O'Dell

The Good Earth by Pearl S. Buck

The Diary of Anne Frank by Anne Frank

Johnny Tremain by Esther Forbes

Roll of Thunder Hear My Cry by Mildred Taylor

The Mid-Wife's Apprentice by Karen Cushman

The Giver by Lois Lowry

Kira-Kira by Cynthia Kadohata

More Teacher's Favorites for Trading Cards

_____

_____

_____

_____

_____

_____

Host a Trading Card Swap

Encourage reading for pleasure by holding a Trading Card Swap with another class. Each student brings a full set of trading cards to swap during the exchange. Appropriate snacks include cups of high-protein snack mix and power punch. The included recipes (page 81) use ingredients that encourage maximum brain functioning.

- Hold a swap in which students prepare cards for any recreational book that they are reading.
- Use classroom sets and have an entire class read the same book or novel and then switch sets with another class. Use the Trading Card Swap to incite interest among students who have not yet read the upcoming book.
- Follow the swap with a recording of one of the books presented that day.
- Videotape some of the students presenting their cards and show it on the school's closed circuit television network to encourage other youngsters to read the books presented.

Bring your cards and come to swap!

At _____

classroom you will stop.

The time is _____, so don't be late.
Our Trading Card Swap is sure to be great!

High-Protein Snack Mix

- 1 large box high-protein oat cereal rings
- 2 cups (480 ml) unsalted peanuts
- 1 cup (240 ml) unsalted, shelled sunflower seeds
- 2 cups (480 ml) raisins
- 1 box small bite-sized wheat biscuits or other high-protein cereal
- Choose one: 1 cup (240 ml) peanut butter, carob or chocolate chips

Mix in a large bowl and serve in paper cups.

Power Punch

Mix equal parts orange juice, ginger ale and pineapple juice. Serve in paper cups.

Trading Card Award

Congratulations to _____

for participating in a Trading Card Swap on

_____
date

in the classroom of _____
teacher

You shared your insights on the book

_____
title

_____
signature of teacher

Name_____ Date _____

Book Chat—For Girls _____

Book Title: _____

Author: _____

Number of Pages: _____

Illustrator: _____

1. I like the way that _____ and _____.

    reacted to one another in the story. This shows characters who _____

    _____

    _____

    _____

2. I would like to be more like _____ in the

    story because of the way that he or she _____

    _____

    _____

    _____

3. From this story, I learned about a way to deal with problems by myself.

    It was _____

    _____

    _____

    _____

    _____

Name_____ Date _____

Book Chat—For Boys

Book Title: _____

Author: _____

Number of Pages: _____

Illustrator: _____

Respond to each item using complete sentences.

1. Pretend you are telling a friend why he or she should read this book. What will you say? _____

   _____

   _____

   _____

2. This character in the book was interesting and smart. I would like to be like _____ in the book because _____

   _____

   _____

   _____

3. This story has a strong plot. The most exciting part was when _____

   _____

   _____

   _____

   _____

Block Center Time

Objective: Students will spend time in the block center each day, using manipulatives to improve spatial skills and to discuss how these spatial tasks can be solved. These block centers will help students improve spatial reasoning skills among girls and help boys use spatial ability to improve verbal skills.

Materials:
- well-stocked block center

Directions:

1. Consider setting aside 30-minute blocks of time in your primary or early elementary classroom's block center to be used for "boy time" or "girl time." This might help to accommodate the girls' need to spend longer periods of uninterrupted time on a block project.

2. Research shows that boys change tasks more frequently than girls. Psychologist Diane McGuinness found that in a 20-minute period, preschool boys did an average of 4.5 different activities, while preschool girls concentrated on just 2.5 different tasks. Moreover, the boys appeared to be more distractible in their play, interrupting their play four times more often to look at something, especially other kids! This makes "gender sense."

3. In addition to the traditional wooden blocks, cycle other kinds of blocks (see the list below) in and out of the block center.

4. Place small dolls, plastic animals, plastic flowers, plastic foods and other housekeeping kinds of items in the block center. This may help boys to practice their verbal skills by setting up block projects that focus on people and places, not just on things. For example, he might set up a garage with a car in it or a house with a family inside or a fruit stand with bananas and apples, instead of the traditional tower to knock over.

Block Center Materials:

- full set of plain wooden blocks
- colored parquetry blocks and pattern cards
- waffle blocks
- Lincoln Logs™
- foam blocks
- cardboard "brick" blocks
- Unifix™ cubes
- Legos™ and other construction blocks
- interlocking plastic rings
- plasic dinosaurs

- plastic farm and zoo animals
- small dolls, plastic fruits and vegetables
- rolling vehicles: cars, trucks, ambulance, fire truck, police car
- empty show boxes with lids*
- oatmeal and salt containers*
- plastic bowls with lids*
- small jewelry boxes with lids*
- empty thread spools*

*Ask parents to save and send these items to school

Questions to Prompt Thinking in the Block Center

A Combination Instructional and Assessment Tool

Student: _____

Teacher: _____ Date:_____

Observations: _____

_____

_____

Response to Questions: _____

_____

_____

Recommendations: _____

_____

Date: _____

Observations: _____

_____

_____

Response to Questions: _____

_____

_____

Recommendations: _____

_____

_____

Use this form with the questions on the next page.

Block Center Questions

1. What can you tell me about your block project today?

_____

2. How are you using the _____ blocks to make this work?

_____

3. Can you think of a way to use the blocks differently?

_____

4. How did you make this happen?

_____

5. Can we add something else to this block project? What can you add?

_____

6. Do you think this will last very long? How can we make it stronger?

_____

7. Tell me about how you built this.

_____

8. Can you think of another kind of block we might use?

_____

9. Did you work by yourself or with other children? Tell me about this.

_____

10. How many blocks did you use? What shapes were they?

_____

11. Did you have any surprises when you were building this?

Name_____ Date _____

Snapshot of My Block Project

picture here

_____
name

Tell me about your block project.

_____

_____

_____

_____

I used _____ number of blocks. The shapes that I used were ____

_____

To make this project better, I would_____

_____

_____

_____

_____

0/1040LE   **87**   Gender-Based Activities

Pattern Card Practice

Objective: Students will practice patterns using blocks.

Materials:
- pattern or parquetry blocks
- preprinted pattern card
- timer
- worksheet

Directions: Pair boys and girls to work on completing pattern card tasks in three-minute intervals. Use a timer to help the children on task. Instruct the children to study the pattern for one minute. Then set the timer for two minutes. The children will take turns selecting the next block to complete the pattern. It is important that both children have an equal number of turns to select the next block to complete the pattern. This makes "gender sense" because girls need to see math at work, and boys need to talk about the way that they see math at work.

88   Gender-Based Activities

Names: _____

and_____

Date: _____ Grade: _____

Pattern Name:_____

Time: _____

The hardest thing about this pattern card was _____

_____

We figured out that _____

_____

It took us the longest to_____

_____

Pattern Name: _____

Time: _____

The hardest thing about this pattern card was _____

_____

_____

We figured out that _____

_____

It took us the longest to_____

_____

_____

More Ideas for Improving Spatial Reasoning While Talking "Math"

Craft Stick Challenge

Objective: Pairs of boys and girls will use craft sticks to complete a set of reasoning tasks and then complete a worksheet that asks them to tell how they solved the challenge.

Materials:
- one box of wooden craft sticks per child
- black or blue paper for work area
- *Craft Stick Challenge* worksheets (page 91)
- pencils

Sample Challenges:

1. Use 15 craft sticks or less to create a house with as many windows as you can.
2. Make a maze with only one way to escape, and use as few craft sticks as you can.
3. Create an octagon with your craft sticks.
4. Design the ideal classroom using your craft sticks.
5. Make your names using the craft sticks.
6. Design a set of stairs with the craft sticks.
7. Use the craft sticks to make a three-dimensional scene.
8. Create a cube showing all sides, using the craft sticks.

Craft Stick Challenge

Names: _____

and _____

Approximate time to complete our task: _____

Our task was _____

We used _____ (number of) craft sticks.

We figured out that _____

_____

It was easier when we _____

_____

To make the task work, we had to _____

_____

(Girl's answer) When I looked at the task, I realized that _____

_____

_____

_____

(Boy's answer) When I looked at the task, I realized that _____

_____

_____

_____

Who Ya Gonna Call? Math Busters

Objective: Boys will improve short-term memory while girls develop problem-solving skills.

Rationale: Pairs of boys and girls use the telephone directory to look up phone numbers, call out the number to one another, dial the number and then write the number on the scratch pad to check it. Boys and girls take turns switching roles as the challenge giver and the "math buster," or the one who solves the task.

This makes "gender sense" because research indicates that boys may be less capable of remembering numbers in sequence, especially when given orally. Girls, on the other hand, seem to appreciate the use of numbers when it is related to a real-life task. All children need to practice sequencing numbers, repeating numbers and writing what they hear.

Materials:

- telephone books
- real (unplugged) telephones for practice
- scratch paper
- pencils
- *Math Busters* worksheets (page 93)

Directions:

1. The challenge giver reads the task. The children work together to find an answer in the telephone directory. They write the answer on the worksheet.
2. The challenge giver then takes the directory and reads the telephone number to the "math buster."
3. The math buster writes the answer on the scratch pad.
4. The math buster dials the number on the telephone, while saying the numbers aloud.
5. The team checks the number that he or she dialed against the correct answer on the worksheet.

Name_____ Date _____

| Challenge 1 | Find a veterinarian who specializes in treating large animals such as pigs and horses. |

Dr. _____ and the number is _____.

Did we get it right on the scratch pad and phone? _____

| Challenge 2 | We want to go on a field trip, but we need to rent a bus for our class. Who can we call? |

The company is _____ and the number is _____.

| Challenge 3 | We want to order an ice cream cake for our teacher's birthday. Who can we call? |

_____ at _____ makes ice cream cakes.

Did we get it right on the scratch pad and phone? _____

| Challenge 4 | Our soccer team needs new shirts with the team name silk-screened on the back. Who can do this job? |

_____ silk-screens shirts. The number is _____.

| Challenge 5 | We need to do a research project at the town library. How can we find out if they are open on Thursday nights? |

The number to call is _____. Our local branch is on _____ Street.

| Challenge 6 | The telephone number for our school is _____. |

Did we get it right?_____

The Shopping Challenge

Objective: Pairs of students use the grocery store sale pages from the newspaper to plan a budget and menu.

Rationale: This activity makes "gender sense" because all children need to practice using mathematics to solve real-life tasks. Girls show skill at computation early on, so they will feel good about this task. Boys need a chance to practice computation and to learn life skills such as planning for events and meals. Again, all children need to learn estimation and budgeting, which happen naturally as one takes the shopping challenge.

Materials:
- grocery store sale pages
- *The Shopping Challenge* worksheets (pages 95-96)
- calculators (for checking work)
- pencils

Directions: Students should complete the Shopping Challenges on pages 95 and 96.

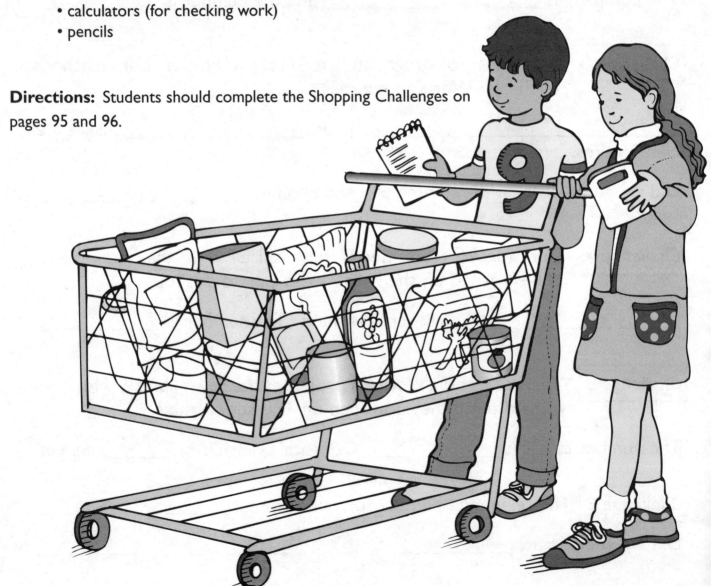

Name_____   Date _____

The Shopping Challenge I

Use the sale page to plan a celebration party for the winners of the school wide Math Bee. There will be 40 students and 10 teachers involved in the party. You have $50 to spend on your party.

Work Area

Items purchased:_____

_____

_____

Price of each item: _____

_____

_____

Amount that we spent:_____

Did we meet our goal?_____

Name_____   Date _____

The Shopping Challenge 2

You need to pack your lunch and your little brother's lunch every school day for one week. Use the sale page to purchase items for the lunches. You have $2 for each person to spend each day. *Bon appetite!*

Work Area

Monday's lunch menu and cost: _____

Tuesday's lunch menu and cost: _____

Wednesday's lunch menu and cost: _____

Thursday's lunch menu and cost: _____

Friday's lunch menu and cost: _____

Total amount spent: _____

Did we meet our goal?_____

Objective: This activity will help boys improve computational skills while helping girls to think quickly when presented with a math reasoning challenge.

Rationale: This activity makes "gender sense" because research suggests that while girls (at least in elementary school) do better than boys on computation tasks, the boys excel in using the reasoning skills required to decide when and how to use a computation skill. Interesting challenge! We need to teach all children how to think on their feet.

Directions: Students will solve mathematical reasoning problems, given orally (see pages 99-100 for sample challenges). Each problem solved correctly will earn a "foot" certificate. Every five "feet" a child earns can be traded in for a reward.

Note: Recently, I observed 28 youngsters who had been selected, through a rigorous testing and competition process, to represent their fourth grade on a district-wide Math Computation Competition team. These were youngsters who can do math quickly! Although my nine-year-old daughter was a participant (and did well), approximately three-fourths of the team members were boys. It was my observation that the boys were aggressive about their answers (right or wrong) and that the boys who were most accurate seemed to do the math in their heads. One teacher-coach (female) lamented: "I just can't get them (the boys) to use the scratch paper." It is also interesting to note that the overall winner in that National Mathcounts competition for 1997 was a seventh grade boy who spoke little English. The young Chinese immigrant demonstrated speed and accuracy as he solved the final challenge, figuring out a payment schedule for a mountain bike purchased for $900. It seemed that this brilliant "mathlete" could see the problem unfolding in his mind. To help girls practice this visual-spatial kind of thinking, we must stimulate that right side of the brain and help them to do math in their minds.

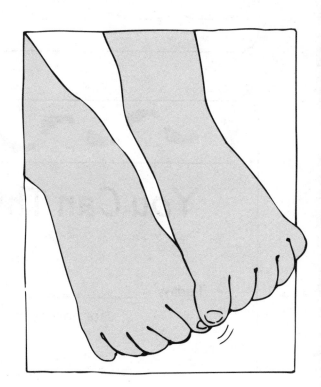

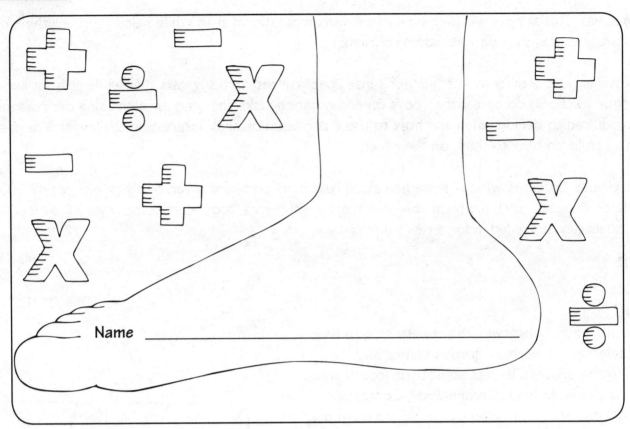

Name _____

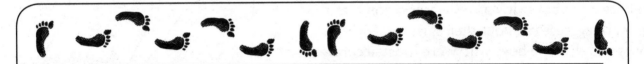

You Can Think on Your Feet!

Today, _____, earned the fifth foot

for solving mathematic reasoning problems.

Teacher: _____

Grade: _____

School: _____

1. Imagine that you have two friends who want to spend the night in your clubhouse with you. How many sleeping bags will you need?
    Answer: three sleeping bags

2. Do you think that a liter of hot water is heavier than a liter of cold water?
    Answer: They weigh the same.

3. If Mark and Chaundra like chocolate milk the best and you and the Anderson twins like white milk the best, do more people like chocolate milk or white milk?
    Answer: white milk

4. How many pairs of tennis shoes will you need for two elephants?
    Answer: four pairs or eight shoes

5. If you have a nickel and four pennies, how much money do you have?
    Answer: nine cents

6. Can you finish this pattern to 0? 12, 11, 10, 9, 8 . . .
    Answer: 7, 6, 5, 4, 3, 2, 1, 0

7. How much is 10 and 2 more?
    Answer: 12

8. What number is smaller than 1?
    Answer: zero

9. If you have eight animal crackers and you eat six, how many will be left?
    Answer: two

10. If it takes you three minutes to ice one cupcake, how long will it take you to ice three cupcakes?
    Answer: nine minutes

11. What is the sum of two quarters, two dimes and five pennies?
    Answer: 75 cents

12. What geometric shape has three sides?
    Answer: triangle

13. What time will it be when the big hand is on the 12 and the little hand is on the 4?
    Answer: four o'clock

14. How many inches are in one foot?
    Answer: 12 inches

15. Andre has 60 pounds of pecans in his wagon. If he shells them all and gets 20 pounds of pecan "meat," how much did the shells weigh?
    Answer: 40 pounds

16. Which would you rather have, six dimes or three quarters?
    Answer: Three quarters is more—75 cents.

17. How many nickels are in 25 cents?
    Answer: five nickels

18. What is the abbreviation for inch?
    Answer: in.

19. Each pizza serves six children. If you have 17 children to feed, how many pizzas will you need?
    Answer: three

20. Which weighs more, a pound of sugar or a pound of salt?
    Answer: They both weigh the same—one pound.

21. In the number 5407, what number is in the 10s place?
    Answer: zero

22. What number comes next in this sequence: 2, 4, 6, 8, ___?
    Answer: 10

Who Was Hypatia?

Objective: Boys and girls will learn to set high expectations for themselves in mathematics.

Rationale: Hypatia of Alexandria is recognized as a mathematician, astronomer and philosopher. She died a tragic death in 415 C.E., murdered by monks who feared her intelligence, saying that she was "devoted at all times to magic, astrolabes and instruments of music." How curious this is, given our present-day knowledge of the fact that the centers for processing mathematics and the centers for musical intelligence are both located in the left side of the brain. It makes sense that gifted mathematicians and musicians would have a lot in common! We can learn from the story of Hypatia, how important it is for both boys and girls to have good role models to look toward as they consider the importance of mathematics.

Directions: Use the following set of *Research Counts* cards (pages 103-106) to involve children in finding out about prominent individuals, past and present, who used mathematics in their discoveries and careers.

Research Counts
Marie Curie

Important Personal Information: _____

_____

_____

How she used mathematics in her work: _____

_____

_____

Her greatest contribution was _____

_____

_____

Research Counts
Albert Einstein

Important Personal Information: _____

_____

_____

_____

How he used mathematics in his work:_____

_____

_____

His greatest contribution was _____

_____

_____

Research Counts
Grace Hopper

Important Personal Information: _____

_____

_____

How she used mathematics in her work: _____

_____

_____

Her greatest contribution was _____

_____

_____

Research Counts
Sir Isaac Newton

Important Personal Information: _____

_____

_____

_____

How he used mathematics in his work:_____

_____

_____

His greatest contribution was _____

_____

_____

Research Counts
Shannon Lucid

Important Personal Information: _____

_____

_____

How she used mathematics in her work: _____

_____

_____

Her greatest contribution was _____

_____

_____

- -

Research Counts
Dr. Percy Julian

Important Personal Information: _____

_____

_____

_____

How he used mathematics in his work:_____

_____

_____

His greatest contribution was _____

_____

_____

Research Counts
Hypatia of Alexandria

Important Personal Information: _____

_____

_____

How she used mathematics in her work: _____

_____

_____

Her greatest contribution was _____

_____

_____

Research Counts
Pythagoras

Important Personal Information: _____

_____

_____

_____

How he used mathematics in his work:_____

_____

_____

His greatest contribution was _____

_____

_____

Research Counts
Individual Incentive

I choose to find out more about _____

_____

This person used mathematics in his or her career to _____

_____

_____

I found out that mathematics counts when one is doing _____

_____

_____

Something that I admire about this individual is _____

_____

Inventions and Inventors

Objective: Using the outline of a male or female scientist, teams of students will fill in the critical information regarding the nature and scope of the scientific invention and its inventor.

Rationale: This activity makes "gender sense" because all children learn best while engaging in the science process skills of classification, recording and analysis of data. However, we know that girls relate best to science when they feel a kinship to the ideas presented. By making the science personal, with the outlines of the scientists as a prop, we can accomplish this goal. Boys, on the other hand, need practice linking the "raw" science to a more pragmatic application ... i.e. "why use it this way?" By linking the inventions with their inventors, we can help boys to recognize the usefulness as well as the curiosity of science.

Materials

- outline of scientist (pages 103-104)
- CD-ROM encyclopedia
- library books
- regular print encyclopedia
- Internet resources (optional)

Directions:

1. The teacher will engage the students with this question: "Which is more important, the invention or the inventor?"
2. The teacher will accept all responses and list them on the overhead or on a sheet of chart paper. (Save these responses for step 10.)
3. The students will practice classification by separating the "invention" responses from the "inventor" responses.
4. The students and teacher will discuss the unique roles of scientists and inventors and then proceed to inquire: "What does it take to become an inventor or scientist?"
5. After this discussion, the teacher will direct the students' attention to the "beaker" with the names of scientists and inventors on it (pages 110-111). The students will be informed that they will have the opportunity to use research tools to find out about the work of male and female scientists and inventors.
6. Each team will select the names of two scientists/inventors from the "beaker."
7. Using the research materials, the teams will classify and analyze data and record it on the appropriate outline of the scientist (pages 112-113).
8. Each team will present its findings to the class.
9. The class will again approach the question: "Which is more important, the invention or the inventor?"
10. The teacher will record these new responses and compare them, with the students, to the earlier responses. The group will inquire as to the nature and scope of these differences.

Teacher as Researcher

Before you do the *Inventions and Inventors* activity, or at the beginning of the school year, ask students to complete page 109. Save the results in a folder. Do not discuss them or draw attention to the gender issue.

After the *Inventions and Inventors* activity, ask children to complete page 109 again. This time, do a tally of the male/female images. Graph the results. Then pull out the drawings from the beginning of the unit. Tally and graph those results. Is there a difference?

With so much discussion about gender sensitivity and diversity in schools, one might think that change would be swift. Think again. Refer again to the activity on page 109. In 40 years of asking students to draw what they think a scientist looks like, little has changed. "In the most recent 'draw a scientist' study, 100% of the boys and 84% of the girls are still drawing men."[1]

Could you change this data? It would be interesting to have some teachers engage students in the task before and after some of the activities, such as *Meet the Scientist* or *Inventions and Inventors*. Do you think you could make a difference?

[1]Sadker, M., and D. Sadker. *Failing at Fairness: How America's Schools Shortchange Girls*. New York: Charles Scribner's Sons, 1994.

What Do You Think?

This Is What I Think a Scientist Looks Like

This Is What I Think a Scientist Does

_____

_____

_____

_____

_____

_____

Marie Curie

Dr. Eleanor Franklin

Barbara McClintock

Sally Ride

Dr. Elizabeth Blackwell

Hypatia of Alexandria

Dr. Sarah Parker

Adah B. Thoms

Dr. Shirley Ann Jackson

Elizabeth Lucas Pinckney

Dr. Benjamin Carson

Thomas Edison

Albert Einstein

Dr. Jonas Salk

Benjamin Banneker

Alexander Graham Bell

Galileo Galilei

Michael Faraday

Robert Boyle

Daniel Bernoulli

Amelia Earhart
Stephanie Kwolek
Mae Carol Jemison
Dr. Lise Meitner
Margaret Mead
Clara Barton
Christa McAuliffe
Rachel Carson
Susan LaFlesche Picotte
Dr. Maria Montessori
Robert Hooke
Sir Isaac Newton
Charles Darwin
Booker T. Washington
Guglielmo Marconi
Pierre Curie
George Washington Carver
The Wright Brothers
Benjamin Franklin
Peregrinus

Female Scientist

Name_____ Date _____

Male Scientist

Name_____   Date _____

Meet a Scientist

Several times each year, invite a man or woman who uses science in his or her career field to visit your classroom. Ask the scientist or science worker to bring in "props" or real tools or examples of his or her work. After the speaker gives his or her demonstration, invite the students to interview the guest.

Scoping Out Science as a Career

What was your favorite subject in school? _____

_____

Why do you enjoy science? _____

_____

How did you stay motivated in high school and college? _____

_____

How do you use science in your work? _____

_____

Do scientists work alone or with others? _____

_____

How could you work toward a career that involves science? _____

_____

Name of our guest: _____

Career field of our guest: _____

Continent Connections

Objective: Students will label each of the seven continents and oceans of the world and draw pictures of the primary natural resources that are used by people on those continents. This activity will help students see the relationships among spatial location of landforms on the Earth, as well as the ways people use natural resources.

Materials
- *Label the Continents* reproducible (pages 116-117)
- atlas
- globe or world map
- CD-ROM encyclopedia or atlas (optional)

Directions:

1. The teacher will begin the discussion with a review of the seven continents. The review will include: showing students the location of the continents on the world map, spelling and writing the names of the continents on the board or overhead and discussing the location of each of the continents in relationship to where the students live.

2. Students will discuss the question: How are the continents the same and different?

3. The students' responses can be listed on chart paper or on page 118.

4. The teacher will bring the class together by telling them that on each continent, geography impacts the ways that people and animals find food and shelter and people make a living. The climate, landforms and location on each continent make a difference.

5. Students and teacher will review *The Continent Connection Task* (page 119). It has two parts: spatial and verbal. In part one, students use resource materials to label the names of the continents along with major rivers and surrounding bodies of water. They also draw symbols or pictures to represent the major resources of each region.

6. In part two, students use their resource books to analyze the impact of climate, landforms and location on the ways that people live in each part of the world.

7. This task will take a minimum of five to six class periods (30 minutes) to complete. It is recommended that teams of two students work on each cognitive connection task.

Label the Continents

_____

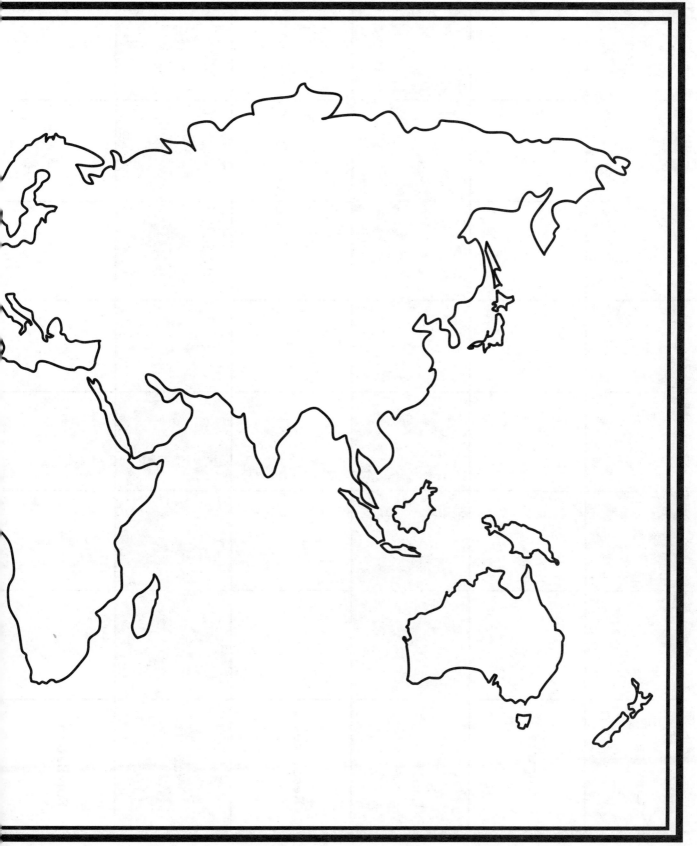

Name _____ Date _____

Continent Connections

Name of Continent	Climate	Landforms	Resources	Water	Population

Name_____   Date _____

The Continent Connection Task

Part 1

Use the two-page map (pages 116 and 117) to fill in the following information:

1. Name of each continent
2. Name and location of each major ocean
3. Names and approximate locations of major rivers
4. Place symbols representing important natural resources such as timber, minerals or wildlife and symbols for major crops on the appropriate continents.

Part 2

1. Complete the *Continent Connections Questionnaire*.
2. Use your atlas, globe, map, and resource materials to find answers to each item on the questionnaire. There may be more than one appropriate answer for the items.
3. Make a list of the resources that you used to complete the questionnaire. Include the title, editor or author, date of publication, and page numbers.

Name_____   Date _____

Continent Connections Questionnaire

1. Based on what you learned about the continents, where would you like to go for a vacation? State your answers in terms of geography and natural resources.

   I would choose to vacation in _____ because of its

   _____

   _____

   _____

2. Using your knowledge of climate and geography, explain why a particular food crop is grown primarily on one of the continents that you learned about.

   The climate of _____ affects the growing of

   _____ because _____

   _____

   _____

3. Geography shapes the way people live. Give one example of the way that people on a particular continent have set up their society or life-style based on geography.

   _____

   _____

   _____

4. Water makes up much of the Earth's surface. Did you find out how much during your research? _____% Given that fact, tell why a particular body of water, an ocean or a river has shaped the way people live in a region of the world. The _____ Ocean/River has shaped life in _____

   because _____

   _____

Resource List

   _____

   _____

   _____

One-Minute Geography Lessons

Boys and girls can benefit from creating *One-Minute Geography Lessons*. These cards are developed by children as a research project, and then used daily to help review for the end of the month Geography Bee. Here is an example of a *One-Minute Geography Lesson* and a reproducible form for you to use with your students (page 122).

Name __Louisa__

One-Minute Geography Lessons

On a favorite television series that *you* can still see today, a silly sailor named Gilligan and his friends were shipwrecked on a body of land that was surrounded on all four sides by water. One of our 50 states, Hawaii, is also a series of these set out in the Pacific Ocean. What do we call a piece of land surrounded on all four sides by water?

Answer __an island__

Name_____ Date _____

One-Minute Geography Lessons

One-Minute Geography Lessons

Answer _____

Exploring Geography

One of the more popular trends in fiction during the past decade has been the emergence of novels depicting life during the dawn of civilization. Titled with intriguing geography-rich names such as *Clan of the Walrus Women*, these stories use the very real knowledge of geography and anthropology to tell how men and women lived in a world that was sparsely settled and constantly changing, environmentally and geologically. It is interesting to note that an important theme in every story is the "strong, intelligent woman." Often a skilled hunter, navigator or shaman, this woman fights for and earns a place of respect in her tribe, group or clan. If she can't, then she moves on and starts her own. Is this a feminist bully pulpit? No. I just think that women are responding to the lack of solid female leaders and explorers that they can look to for inspiration. Clearly, the demands of child-rearing and homemaking were such that they kept women (for the most part) closer to home than to the rivers, seas and trails that might have led them to recognition as explorers. But there were a lot of women who did contribute to geographical exploration. At the same time, many men led fascinating treks that have given us marvelous knowledge of geography today. A good way for children to grasp geography is to explore the lives and work of those who held a life-long fascination for the world around them. Use the *Exploring Geography* cards (pages 124-126) to prepare short class presentations.

Exploring Geography Cards

I Learned About Narcissus Whitman

She was an explorer during the period of _____

and explored the region of_____

Her life was changed by geography in the following ways: _____

_____

_____

One of her contributions was _____

_____

_____

I Learned About Erik the Red

He was an explorer during the period of _____

and explored the region of_____

His life was changed by geography in the following ways: _____

_____

_____

One of his contributions was_____

_____

_____

Exploring Geography Cards

I Learned About Sacajawea

She was an explorer during the period of _____

and explored the region of_____

Her life was changed by geography in the following ways: _____

_____

_____

One of her contributions was _____

_____

_____

- -

I Learned About Lewis and Clark

They were explorers during the period of _____

and explored the region of_____

Their lives were changed by geography in the following ways:_____

_____

_____

One of their contributions was _____

_____

_____

Name_____ Date _____

Exploring Geography Cards

I Learned About _____

She was an explorer during the period of _____

and explored the region of_____

Her life was changed by geography in the following ways: _____

_____

_____

One of her contributions was _____

_____

_____

- -

I Learned About _____

He was an explorer during the period of _____

and explored the region of_____

His life was changed by geography in the following ways: _____

_____

_____

One of his contributions was_____

_____

_____

Jump the Synapse Game

Objective: This activity will increase neural connections by accessing boys' natural sense of competitiveness and girls' love of language.

Materials:
- colored paper
- white paper
- colored, scented markers
- brain pattern

Directions: Cut out 50 "brains" using the pattern provided (page 128). Use green or purple paper to facilitate creativity and flexibility if the teacher is crafting the items, or let students create the items using white paper and scented, colored markers.

Design a question and answer game in which students must identify the right answer to a question by locating it on one of the "brains" in their pile or in the team pile. They flip the "answer" over and ask the next question. Players must attend to the question and select from the answers in the pile of brains. This game can be done with any topic or subject at any grade level. It draws on mental scaffolding.

Example: Start the game with a card with a question or challenge:

> Name one of the three states of matter

Students look through their "pile" or stack for the correct answer. It would be:

> Solid
> Liquid
> or Gas

After answering, the student would flip the "brain" over and ask the next question to the group:

> Which state is water found in when frozen?

This would lead to a new brain with the answer of:

> Solid

The "Jump the Synapse" game continues until all brains are accounted for. Students can create the brains as a chapter review and then quiz one another for the test.